THE SEVENFOLD PATH

THE SEVENFOLD PATH

A Traveler's Guide to Jewish Wisdom

SHIRA MILGROM
WITH DAVID M. ELCOTT

BLOOMSBURY ACADEMIC
NEW YORK • LONDON • OXFORD • NEW DELHI • SYDNEY

BLOOMSBURY ACADEMIC

Bloomsbury Publishing Inc, 1359 Broadway, New York, NY 10018, USA
Bloomsbury Publishing Plc, 50 Bedford Square, London, WC1B 3DP, UK
Bloomsbury Publishing Ireland, 29 Earlsfort Terrace, Dublin 2, D02 AY28, Ireland

BLOOMSBURY, BLOOMSBURY ACADEMIC and the Diana logo are trademarks of Bloomsbury Publishing Plc

First published in the United States of America 2026

Copyright © Shira Milgrom and David M. Elcott, 2026

For legal purposes the Acknowledgments on pp. xvi–xvii constitute an extension of this copyright page.

Cover design: Diana Nuhn
Cover image © Gettyimages.com / Toni Faint

All rights reserved. No part of this publication may be: i) reproduced or transmitted in any form, electronic or mechanical, including photocopying, recording or by means of any information storage or retrieval system without prior permission in writing from the publishers; or ii) used or reproduced in any way for the training, development or operation of artificial intelligence (AI) technologies, including generative AI technologies. The rights holders expressly reserve this publication from the text and data mining exception as per Article 4(3) of the Digital Single Market Directive (EU) 2019/790.

Bloomsbury Publishing Inc does not have any control over, or responsibility for, any third-party websites referred to or in this book. All internet addresses given in this book were correct at the time of going to press. The author and publisher regret any inconvenience caused if addresses have changed or sites have ceased to exist, but can accept no responsibility for any such changes.

Library of Congress Cataloging-in-Publication Data

ISBN: HB: 979-8-8818-4262-8
ePDF: 979-8-7651-6390-0
eBook: 979-8-7651-6389-4

Typeset by Integra Software Services Pvt. Ltd.
Printed and bound in the United States of America

For product safety related questions contact productsafety@bloomsbury.com.

To find out more about our authors and books visit www.bloomsbury.com and sign up for our newsletters.

To
Cruv, Oren, Sela,
Rimon, Dami, Mira,
Lefett, Maya, Romy, and Ezra

To whom we bequeath a precious world
ever more in need of their
tenderness and courage

> There is nothing new under the sun.
> *Ecclesiastes*

> **It is within a person's power
> to renew everything.**
> *Yehudah Aryeh Leib Alter, Sefat Emet*

CONTENTS

Preface xi
Acknowledgments xvi
The Sevenfold Path: An Introduction 1

1   Tzelem Elohim / A Spark of the Divine   19

    A LIFE ON PURPOSE
    You Are Alive for a Reason

2   Brit / Covenant   33

    A LIFE OF CONNECTION
    Learning to Love

3   Teshuva / Healing and Return   49

    A LIFE OF INNER GROWTH
    The Courage to Become You

4   Kedusha / The Sacred   87

    A LIFE OF WONDER
    Nourishing a Heart of Gratitude

5   Makom / The Presence   97

    A LIFE OF OPENNESS
    We Are Never Alone

6 Tzedaka / Justice 113

   A LIFE OF RESPONSE
   Reaching beyond the Self

7 Shabbat 125

   A LIFE OF JOY
   Heaven on Earth

Coda 141
Appendix Exploring Jewish Ritual Life: Traditions for the 21st Century 143
Notes 169
Index 171
About the Authors 172

PREFACE

We came of age in the late sixties and early seventies, a tumultuous time of violence, challenges to the existing norms and values, and also a time of great hope in the future. Judaism brought us together at summer camp, all that youthful energy celebrating the intense life that summer camp offers. Friendship blossomed into a more serious relationship, filled with excitement yet fraught with all the anxieties that love brings. We were certainly contrasts, one very dark, loud, and wild Mediterranean from semirural California, the other blond, a rabbi's daughter brought up in segregated Virginia, studious, introspective, and conservative. But there was music and dance and wanderlust to explore the world, devouring languages and cultures with unlimited possibility. Despite differences in style and substance, the core we shared was grounded in Jewish life and a vision of a loving, creative family adventure.

We were both PhD graduate students, political psychology and linguistics, working part time and then, in but six years, filling our home with four children as well. We were convinced that we could handle it all, naive twenty-somethings that we were. Exhausted for sure, but our Jewish home of Shabbat and holidays, extended family and friends joining in, was filled with laughter and joy. We were on the path, albeit a rocky and often chaotic one, that we had envisioned when we married. Living Jewish was an anchoring and often calming resource. In so many ways, this book is an outgrowth of the world we struggled to create.

Driving down a Los Angeles freeway one afternoon, Shira turned and said, "Had I been born ten years later, I might have become a rabbi." I answered, "Why not now?" Pregnant with our fourth child, Shira called Hebrew Union College the next day and began the application process that would lead to rabbinical school, uprooting our family of young kids, flying from Los Angeles to New York with Mutti, the great-grandmother, in tow. We never left. Shira graduated and became the rabbi of Congregation Kol Ami for thirty-seven years. Our children flourished and, as goslings do, flew off to their own adventures of world travel, lengthy studies, marriages, and now, many years later, sharing with us our ten grandchildren.

Serving as a rabbi in one synagogue for so long, three generations of births and deaths, students who themselves become parents at the synagogue preschool, meant exploring and experimenting with how faith can make life meaningful, purposeful, joyful, and creative. What Shira learned was that to succeed, a rabbi must let go of the trappings of authority, of being all-knowing, of speaking from high on the pulpit. There is so much wisdom out there to be brought into the world of the synagogue, and not just from outside scholars and artists.

Churches, temples, synagogues, and mosques are overflowing with so much life experience and learning, talent and insight. We opened our home to the outside world, sitting with friends and congregants at our Sabbath table, inviting what became hundreds and hundreds into our outdoor sukkah, the festival booth that reminds us of our fragility, singing and celebrating in multiple languages, welcoming so many different cultures and life experiences. At the synagogue, it often meant singing together, me on the guitar, in joyful harmonies at Shabbat services—even during those early pandemic months when the two of us streamed Shabbat morning services from our home. Our world was filled with stories overflowing, some of great happiness, others of pain and sorrow. A core vision of this book, that each human being is an image of God, of infinite value and uniqueness, became a hallmark of Shira's many decades as a rabbi and our shared partnership at Kol Ami, being part of a vibrant community.

And I had to learn the same truths about effective leadership, slowly, over many years, that the role of a teacher, a spiritual guide, is to help nurture possibilities, to model a willingness to change course and grow, to see the world as a place of adventure. And to listen attentively and with empathy to the stories told in settings across the continent, in what often felt like God-forsaken places around the world, and now in the maximum-security prison where I teach incarcerated men who are passionate about learning as part of their college degree program. These men are a touchstone for me, confirming the core Jewish belief that change, growth, and renewal are always possible.

But it is not easy. The Hassidic master Nachman of Bratislav, who lived centuries ago, a man who struggled his whole life with shame and fear, left us with an image, a pathway to move forward: "The whole world is a very narrow bridge, and the essence of life is to not be overwhelmed with fear." To walk this path is to look into the mirror and imagine the person I could be, on a journey to becoming whole. And perhaps it is there that the anxiety and fear haunt, that I may die and no one will notice. Or what they notice is not who I really am, or that I am unworthy of being noticed. Reconnecting to our life's story, to a life of meaning and purpose, is not easy work. Seeing it in front of me—looking deeply in the mirror—takes courage. And so we write not only of blessing and wonder, but also with the realization that being human, crossing the narrow bridge of life, is hard work.

At the same time, whether meditating in a jungle monastery, on-the-feet joyfully clapping at a Black Baptist church, volunteering on an impoverished island, joining arm in arm with so many ethnic, national, and religious friends to fight for justice, what became clear to us is that we are grounded in Jewish. Jewish text and language, crazy and often joyous traditions, an immersive fabric of being, all led to vibrant Jewish celebration at the core of our lives. Being Jewish is not the only way to be—the world overflows with creative forces, with deep and wondrous faith, with the magic of glorious sunrises and sunsets and, above all, with love. Among the many gifts of being alive, love, being loved, love in relationship, love in commitment—love is the greatest gift of all.

Judaism is one path, an exuberant journey, among the many available to all of us.

Hopefully this book is a launchpad for your own spiritual exploration, one stop on your life journey. Perhaps Judaism serves as your unique pathway; perhaps you are curious to explore Judaism as one path in a world of many choices. Perhaps you simply want to dip a toe into the world of the spirit. We are mortal, but between birth and death there is so much possible, so much joy and celebration, so much to learn, absorb, and experience. You have also undoubtedly already experienced sorrows and disappointments. There is love and loss ahead for each of us. Hopefully, in the stories and images of past generations and the newer ones gathered over these past decades, this book will provide not only solace but deep meaning and joy.

Years ago, we spent a weekend at a retreat with a famous Yemenite dance teacher, Margalit Oved. We whirled on our feet and were taught how to tell stories just with our hands. She told us that she was a bearer of the stories and life experiences of her ancestors. "I had two grandmothers. One lived to be 99 years old, the other to 101. They wrote a book called *The Wisdom of Life*. Each day of their lives was a page in the book. "Don't look for the book in any library." Margalit laughed and said, "I swallowed it."

So many words have been written in the past, great books of wisdom, spiritual and psychological guides. No doubt, many more will be written as we humans delve deeper into the mysteries of the universe. For now, dive into these pages, the foundational texts and spiritual expansions, the legends and stories, the prayers and rituals, and swallow them all; store them as part of your life journey, and know that the universe—and you—exist for a purpose to be explored, nurtured, and blessed.

David M. Elcott

ACKNOWLEDGMENTS

This book began its life as a short loose-leaf guide to a Jewish spiritual life. Richard Brown, the energetic and curious religion editor at Bloomsbury, saw in that guide the possibility of a book that might speak to the heart of seekers of many traditions. It would not have seen the light of day without the skill, expertise, and attentive shepherding of his team—Victoria Shi, Anne Hunt, Matt Evans and Linda Kessler—and others behind the scenes. We owe them each a debt of gratitude.

The night sky is thick with stars. I have been blessed by so many teachers of Judaism—and some of them stand out even amid a star-studded sky. Rabbi Harold Schulweis taught me that Judaism wasn't a narrow discipline of text and religion, but that it encompasses all the complexity of the human psyche. Rabbi Yitz and Blu Greenberg taught me that traditional Jewish observance is rich with emotion and humanity. Rabbi Larry Kushner opened the door to Jewish mysticism; that door, as it turns out, opened into my life and all life around me. Rabbi Larry Hoffman taught me to listen deeply and speak the truth.

From my congregation of thirty-seven years, Congregation Kol Ami, I learned that a community of joy, courage, honesty, and vulnerability is not a mirage or a pipe dream; it is real and life sustaining.

All of us participate in eternity. I am blessed to know that I do. My parents, Jacob and Jo, implanted within me a lifelong love of Torah;

its words and poetry formed the cadences of my childhood and are etched in my soul. My parents-in-law, Ruth and Eddie, modeled a marriage of fearless loving. David, my husband, taught me that love could be trusted (not easy). We have been travelers together since the beginning of time. The homes our four children have created are filled with joy and gratitude and excitement, celebration and courage, and powerful loving. One of our older grandchildren read a final draft of this book. "I laughed and I cried," she said. "This is my life and the Judaism I live."

There really are few words to express the depth of gratitude that I feel. The tears that fill my eyes at this moment are a better tribute. I see it! I see the gift—this participation in eternity, even for a moment. For the privilege of learning and living and loving—for seeing and passing it on—I am endlessly grateful.

Shira Milgrom

The Sevenfold Path: An Introduction

In his book, *Love, Medicine and Miracles*, Dr. Bernie Siegel describes a moment in his kitchen when the garbage disposal got stuck. He calls out to his wife, "What do I do now?" "Press the reset button!" she calls back. Bernie then turns to God, "God, why didn't you give us a reset button?" "I did," says God. "I gave you pain and suffering."[1] However we understand our own pain and struggle, we know that times of suffering hold the possibility of reset; we reevaluate who we are, what matters most in our lives, and how we want to live.

Sometimes suffering is shared. In 2020, the world was plunged into a global pandemic; life as we knew it came to a sudden halt. We wanted that moment to be such a turning point, an opportunity for reset. But instead, the years that have followed have continued to fuel our sense of crisis. Political upheaval, environmental degradation, and the lingering anxieties of global pandemics have upended the foundations that we have taken for granted and upon which we have built our lives. The world that we have constructed is no longer as we had expected.

As we write, religions are providing the fuel for inconceivable brutality and oppression. They are justification for taking away human and civil rights; they are used to validate racism, misogyny, and ethnic hatred; indeed, murder is once again rationalized as doing God's will. Painful for us, so many of the policies of the State of Israel and its Jewish majority have proven no exception. It is now all the more essential to anchor ourselves in a Jewish wisdom of compassion and empathy, celebrating the diversity that honors the Divine in all life. The Judaism that we know and practice is centered in love.

This book is a response to this moment. Instead of falling back into complacency, we could let this moment open us up and peel us back. Born of our vulnerability, we join in a spiritual search, a longing to name and connect with what matters most. We are gifted this opportunity, to be vulnerable and to see what is exposed underneath, to understand that we are connected to all of life, that we are responsible to others and to the life around us. We are being given the chance for a reset—what is also called a spiritual awakening.

In spite of all the conflict and violence that religions have brought into the world, we can't wish religion away. Religion won't go away—ever. Religion—in its purest, most spiritual forms—is the way we name the mystery and majesty of the world of which we are a part. It is the way we acknowledge the realness of spiritual energy: why we love in the face of death, why we hope in the face of despair, why we need our lives to matter. It is our conviction that we are not alone and that we share in and are connected to an infinite universe.

Religions are spiritual alphabets. They give us a language with which to explore the spiritual dimensions of the universe and with which to sculpt the spiritual dimensions of our own lives. Languages—and cultures—may share a deep structure, but each is unique. So, too, with religions. Each religion offers its own way to mine and shape the spiritual life. One way we express this spiritual longing is by telling our stories. Stories speak the language of the soul; they are a direct connection to what matters most for each of us—even when we don't know what that is. Finding our story—giving voice to our story—connects us to our deepest selves.

ON STORIES

Religions have stories of such majesty and grandeur: Moses coming down Mount Sinai with the Ten Commandments, Siddhartha abandoning the palace to become Gautama Buddha, Jesus on the path to crucifixion and resurrection, Muhammad fleeing Mecca to found Islam. Whole civilizations have been built on these stories.

"But I don't have a story," you are thinking. Barbara Meyerhoff, in her 1976 anthropological study of senior adults in Venice Beach, California, *Number Our Days*, convened small groups of elders in a workshop called "Living History." She encouraged them to tell their stories. One of the participants, an eighty-eight-year-old Russian refugee whose family was lost to her, was sure she had no story to tell. Whatever good there may have been, it had been long buried under the weight of the suffering. But as she began to talk, she began to remember. She said,

> When I first heard about this group, I thought to myself, What can I learn? What can I hear that I don't know, about life in the Old Country, of the struggles, the life in the poor towns, in the bigger

towns, of the rich people and the poor people? What is there to learn, I'm eighty-eight, that I haven't seen myself? Then I think, What can I give to anybody else? I'm not an educated woman. It's a waste of time. That was my impression. But then I came here and heard all those stories. I knew them, but you know it was laid down deep, deep in your mind, with all those troubles mixed. You know it's there but you don't think of it, because sometimes you don't want to live in your past. Who needs all these foolish stories? But finally, all the pictures came up. It was laying on them like layers, separate layers of earth, and all of a sudden in this class I feel it coming up like lava. It just melted away the earth from all those people and they became alive. And then to me it looked like they were never dead. "I have nothing to say," I think. But I start to say it and the memories come up in me like lava. So I felt I enriched myself. And I am hoping maybe I enriched somebody else. All this, it's not only for us. It's for the generations.[2]

When we are separated from that which animates our lives, we have difficulty tapping into our stories. We deeply know that everyone has a story.

The great stories did not happen to the masters of old. They happen to us. You and me. This moment. A tale unfolds. It is only that we have lost the narrative element of our existence. How could my life possibly be a spiritual tale? I must surely be a secular drone. But even that confession is the nucleus of a spiritual tale! If Moses, our teacher, had your definition of spiritual, he would have remained an Egyptian, too. Never entered the wilderness. For you see, we are the stories.

And for this reason there can be no honest telling about holy encounters without sharing them in their context. All true theology must finally be personal. God meets one of us.³

And so, we open with a story.

The Ferry Ride

Late summer, now many decades ago, a first-year rabbinic student and pregnant with our daughter Liore, I was on a ferry from Victoria Island to Seattle together with David—a long four-hour trip. I was somewhat aggravated with myself because I had left behind a book on the Jewish High Holiday liturgy, from which I hoped I would learn more about specific prayers and from which I might derive inspiration for the coming Days of Awe. Oh well, I had left it behind.

David and I found ourselves seated opposite two older women, in a corner without much of a view. Conversation with me those days easily centered on children. "Is this your first?" "No, it's my fourth." And in the course of this initial exchange, one of the women told us proudly that she had fourteen grandchildren and seventeen great-grandchildren, all of this, she told us, from four children. One of her children had had one child of her own and then had adopted three more: an abused boy of two, a handicapped child, and a Vietnamese baby. Another, the mother of six, took in neighboring children with learning and emotional disabilities. We commented that her household must have been one of a great deal of love to have generated such love in the homes of her children.

And she began to tell us about the love in her home, the love that she finds in Jesus. She asked if we were Jewish, and proceeded to say that she was not interested in convincing us of anything—and just continued.

She talked about a childhood of poverty, about having boarded with a warmhearted Jewish family, and the next thing I remember, she told us that after having given birth to her fourth child she was diagnosed with terminal tuberculosis—too sick to be sent to a sanatorium, so sick that she was left to die. She spoke of her anguish that she would not live to raise her own children. For me, one of my greatest fears had been that I, too, wouldn't live to raise my children (a fear long since relieved, now being a grateful grandmother of ten). She talked, and I cried. She was not upset by my crying; she hardly seemed to notice it. It seemed normal and understood to her. She told us how they came to take her children away—the first two to the East, and then they came for the toddler and the baby. She spoke, also, about the growth of her faith in Jesus, a process which she claims was the source of her healing. She spoke about the point in those months when she could finally accept that she was worthy of being loved—for her, worthy of Divine Love.

She lived. She lived to gather her children from the four corners of the earth and raise them to adulthood and to lives of love. What I remember most was the depth of her feelings and her willingness to share them with me. Her humanity. And I remember her deep faith.

As I sat listening to her, crying, I thought to myself ironically that I could have been reading *about* the High Holiday liturgy, I could have been reading *about* spirituality—instead of experiencing it.

Adonai, al tashlicheinu milfanecha, v'ruach kodsh'cha al tikach mimenu.
God, don't send me away from You
And do not take your spirit of holiness away from me.

This desperate plea is among my most favorite prayers, a refrain of the High Holidays.

On that crowded old ferry, an older, Jesus-loving Christian grandmother met a young, pregnant Jew, and we transcended difference, experiencing the miracle of God's Presence. Two human beings, face-to-face, each an image of God. So begins the first chapter, **Tzelem Elohim/A Spark of the Divine**, teaching us that **You Are Alive for a Reason, A LIFE ON PURPOSE.**

You have your stories—your own direct links to the sacred.

If only we reached out, we would not be alone, so that between us, among us, we could see the face of God. We are not strangers to one another. What we can share are our stories. If only we allow ourselves to reframe, to peek at the world differently, we could together witness God's Presence: stories of soul and spirit, moments of our lives when we have felt guided, times when we have known that we were in a certain place for a reason, or when we have felt the presence of someone long gone from this earth, or times we have experienced a renewal of purpose and our reason for being.

Chapter 2, **Brit/Covenant**, explores relationship and commitment. **A LIFE OF CONNECTION—Learning to Love** is a central aspect of being human.

We believe that life is not accidental. We believe that life breathes with purpose. We believe that you, too, are on purpose. You are not here by accident. We are each alive for a reason. And it is the holy task of each one of us to find out why we are alive. We do not believe in a random, accidental universe. And in telling stories, we realize that we can mine the common and humdrum to tap into the miracles—of love, of wonder, of joy, of purpose and meaning. Together, our stories, the human story, offer transcendence, a peek at eternity.

Butterflies

One year, on a fall day, we received news that one of our closest friends had died. Lil lived into her nineties. She spoke her mind, she had the mouth of a sailor, and she taught our kids to play poker; she was a brilliant therapist and a force for good in our lives. We sat on the couch at home, and the grief welled up in us. Staring out the window, we saw a rush of leaves, thirty, forty, fifty—we couldn't count them—suddenly falling from a tree. But then we realized that there was no tree overhead and that they weren't leaves; they were butterflies.

Coincidence—or grace. This is a choice.

We're telling you these stories to get your attention. And because they are beautiful. And simple. And because the people who experience them know that they are signs of mystery and grace. And because it doesn't matter if it's ferries or butterflies. And because you have your stories—your own direct links to the sacred.

Spiritual Practice / Ritual

Telling our stories.

Without our stories, our spirit dries up. Our stories connect us to where we came from; they tell us why we are here; they tell us to whom and to what we belong; they tell us why we matter. Stories connect us to our souls, to our deepest selves.

You have a story to tell, perhaps one you have never told or written about. It is a story from your life, your tradition, your experience. This ritual will be yours to own or to share if you choose, with family or with a community of friends.

> Please take a few minutes and let your mind float over years of your life.
> Note three or four moments or events that you remember at this moment. They don't have to be earth shattering or monumental, but meaningful to you. Write them down.

> Now that you have recalled these moments in your life, think about the ways they might be connected. There is no correct answer to this question: it is a question of the meaning that you alone can make.
> There may be a profound spark of insight or humor enough to make you laugh. Perhaps it is pain that connects these moments, or extraordinary joy or the warmth of comfort.

> The stories of our inheritance
> What have you learned from your parents
> that you would want the next generation to know?

What have you learned from your parents that you would not want to pass on to the next generation?

What have you learned in your life that you want the next generation to know?

It is hard to be fully human, hard to always know how to be in the world. Chapter 3 on our journey gives us **Teshuva/Healing and Return**, an opportunity for us to focus on **A LIFE OF INNER GROWTH**, using the stories and texts to help us gain **The Courage to Become You.**

ON USING SACRED STORIES

Many years ago, when we still lived in California, we hosted a group of sixth-graders in the sukkah in our backyard. (We celebrate the harvest holiday of Sukkot each fall by building a temporary hut.) David stood up on a chair, pointed to an apple hanging from the roof of the sukkah, and asked the kids, "Where does this apple come from?" And in one voice, the kids answered. You might be thinking "the supermarket"—which wouldn't have been a bad answer—but no, they said, in one voice, "God!" David said, "That's what they teach you in school—that the apple comes from God?" Laughing somewhat nervously, they said, "No—the apple comes from a tree." "And where does the tree come from?" David asked them. And they said, in one voice, "From God." What has happened here? These sixth-grade religious school students knew to turn off their minds the moment they step into their religious school settings. They give the required pat answers that religious instruction seems to require—and they disconnect from everything real that they know. For them, religion has nothing to do with real life. Everything religious has become trivialized and irrelevant.

The story is told about the man who is hiking in the mountains and, walking on a tricky precipice, he loses his balance and slips off the path. As he falls, he grabs the roots of a tree that are jutting out from the edge of the cliff. He hangs on with all his might and calls out, "Can anybody help me?" And then he hears a voice calling from the sky, "You can let go. I will be there for you." A pause—and the man calls out, "Anybody else out there?"

We identify with this man. "You can let go" doesn't make sense to us either. How do we read our sacred stories? What do we do about the splitting of the sea, or a burning bush, or the creation of the universe in seven days? If a story is in our sacred scriptures (whichever that scripture is), does that mean it is true?

"Is it true?" We answer that question by looking at the language of dreams. Think for a moment about a dream you had (that you can remember well). Question: Was the dream true? We venture that you would say probably not. So now, a different question: Did the dream have truths in it? And you would probably answer yes. That is why you still remember it.

From Shira, a story of dreams: When I was a child of seven or eight, I dreamed that my family was having a picnic on the beach. We were sitting on a blanket on the sand, looking at the ocean. Oddly, the ocean began with a wall of water (this was way before the fabulous aquariums we have now—with gigantic glass walls). The wall of water just stayed put; it didn't threaten to flood the beach. As I sat on the beach, I could see the legs of people swimming; I could see jellyfish undulating through the water. And then I saw my brother in the water—drowning! I wanted to yell, but I couldn't find my voice. I looked around—and no one was noticing this, and I couldn't get their attention. Was the dream true? No! Oceans don't start that way, with a wall—and my brother didn't drown in the ocean. It wasn't until many decades later, a parent of children myself, that I understood the dream. Yes, my brother had been drowning; and yes, in some way I had seen it; and yes, no one else had noticed it; and yes, I was powerless to alert them.

Torah—sacred stories—speak in the language of dreams. We can easily dismiss sacred stories by saying that seas don't split like that, bushes don't burn and remain unharmed, the world was not created in seven days—these stories cannot be true! We could dismiss them (as I might have dismissed my dream), but we will miss the extraordinary power in them; we will miss the truths that they carry.

The Zohar, the central work of Jewish mysticism, teaches us: If you look at the garment on the Torah and you think that is the real Torah, woe to you. And if you look at the parchment, and you think that is the real Torah, woe to you. And even if you look at the stories of the Torah and think that they are the whole Torah—you have missed the whole thing. It is perhaps like looking at a person. If you look at her—or him—and only see the clothing or the jewelry and think that is the person, woe to you. And if you think it's the hair color, or skin, or the voice, once again you have missed the person.

Sacred stories deal with the great passages of time and life—the transitions from childhood to old age: birth, death, marriage, and personal transformation. Religion—each in its own way—addresses the one question that science does not: For what purpose? For what purpose was the universe created? For what purpose is there life? Religion comes to ask: Why am I alive? It is a question we cannot afford to live without.

Judaism tells its stories of sacred purpose in its Torah.

"The Torah is ancient Israel's distinctive record of its search for God. It attempts to record the meeting of the human and the Divine, the great moments of encounter. Therefore, the text is often touched by the ineffable Presence. The Torah tradition testifies to a people of extraordinary spiritual sensitivity. God is not the author of the text, the people are; but God's voice may be heard through theirs if we listen with open minds."[4]

The spiritual journey we are on can lead us beyond the limits of our own lifetime. The faith we seek leads us to compassionate connection to all of life and to a sense of responsibility to act on its behalf, not for power, not for control, not for domination. The faith we seek leads us to the courage to love in the face of inevitable loss and to profound gratitude that we are alive at all. The faith we seek connects us to our reason for being and, we pray, to the Source of all Being.

All of life pulses with meaning. This is our religious bias. You are DNA and muscles and atoms and synapses—and we share a huge part of that genetic heritage with the rest of life here on this planet. And you are also intellect and mind and soul—you are also the spirit that animates the rest of your being, that graces you with purpose, and that breathes life into the days with which you have been blessed.

When we connect with the stories that animate our lives with purpose, we also connect to the sacred within all life. Chapter 4, **Kedusha/The Sacred**, brings us to **A LIFE OF WONDER, Nourishing a Heart of Gratitude.**

And what about that burning bush? The poet Elizabeth Barrett Browning wrote,

"Earth's crammed with heaven
And every common bush afire with God
But only he who sees takes off his shoes
The rest sit round and pluck blackberries."

ON WISDOM

On purpose. We are alive for a reason. Love. Wonder. Joy. These values form the foundation of this book. Each section of this book opens with a foundational Jewish value, a prism through which to see the world. Each of these values or concepts is supported by stories: by sacred, scriptural stories and by personal stories—and by spiritual wisdom that is distilled from these stories. Last, each value is connected to a spiritual practice—a way to walk the path of life. These spiritual practices are rituals, ways to tap into the power of life.

There is no end to religious traditions, spiritual wisdom, and philosophical insight. There are way more than seven foundational concepts in Judaism; there are enough sacred stories, whether scriptural or personal, to fill all the libraries of the world, and more spiritual wisdom than the universe can contain. Judaism alone offers countless rituals and blessings. These are but a few. But they are foundational.

ON RITUALS

Wisdom. Stories. Rituals.

We offer a few of Judaism's beautiful rituals in this book, all of which are open to you. We also hope that you will find and cultivate your own rituals that will provide connection and continuity for you. Traditions don't need the weight of history to be meaningful, says Michael Norton, a professor of business administration at Harvard and the author of *The Ritual Effect*. He adds that families who have rituals "report being more likely to brave the hectic travel and traffic to actually gather."[5] Those who don't have such rituals, he found, are less likely to come together.

Judaism's way lies in its pairing of spiritual wisdom with ritual, with an action, a behavior, for spirit alone is not enough. There is no essential Jewish value that doesn't find its expression in a practice, a ritual. Historically, this system of behaviors evolved into its own independent structure, the Jewish legal framework known as halakha. It rests on the Divine nature of revealed scripture (Torah) and on the authority of rabbis who over the centuries have interpreted and expanded the law according to an intricate and clearly articulated system of legal reasoning. The halakha stands on its own as the reason for Jewish practice and behavior and, indeed, has generated powerful allegiance to a religious practice and created strong bonds among its adherents.

This isn't working for much of the world.

On one hand, religion is often being used to fuel fundamentalist nationalism, which does little to address the life of the spirit. More significantly, we know that religious practice is on the wane around the world. Though two-thirds of Americans say they believe in God, only 20 percent attend weekly religious services. Pew Research Center's study "Jewish Americans in 2020" noted that fully 85 percent of American Jews do not consider observing Jewish law as essential to their Jewishness. In 2025, the surgeon general in America, a medical professional, declared a spiritual crisis, a crisis of alienation, of mental health. So, if we are to heal as a society and provide meaning beyond frenetic activity, we need a new way to create a vibrant personal spiritual practice built on the foundations of wisdom and rituals we have inherited.

We need to be open to the world, not cloistered in a religious life separate from all that is around us. The life of the spirit enables us to experience what in chapter 5 is **Makom/The Presence** that is everywhere, beckoning us to **A LIFE OF OPENNESS**, to know that **We Are Never Alone**.

There is so much wisdom available, so many spiritual traditions into which we can tap. Yet it seems that chasing from one to another will not fill a void of meaning. We may want to embrace humanity, but it is also crucial to ground oneself, to explore deeply, to immerse oneself in the particular. While we include other wonderful traditions as we search for life's meaning, this book grounds itself in the Jewish experience.

We cannot ignore that we live in a broken world, a world that needs our engagement, our compassion, a world where we must be **Reaching beyond the Self**. Chapter 6 brings us to **Tzedaka/Justice** that asks for **A LIFE OF RESPONSE**, understanding that we are all partners with God in repairing the world.

Jewish tradition debates whether learning or action is more important. We know that being human requires both. Judaism's learning is endless, a realization that can be overwhelming. The Torah itself cautions us against this all-too-real obstacle:

> This teaching that I give you this day is not too overwhelming for you, nor is it beyond reach. It is not in the heavens, that you should say, "Who among us can go up to the heavens and get it for us and impart it to us, that we may observe it?" Neither is it beyond the sea, that you should say, "Who among us can cross to the other side of the sea and get it for us and impart it to us, that we may observe it?"
>
> No! This is very close to you, in your mouth and in your heart, to observe it.
>
> Deuteronomy 30:11–14

The life-giving waters of Jewish wisdom flow beneath our feet to all who seek a path, right where we live. We need a way to draw up these waters—a way to hold them—in order to irrigate and nourish our lives. Rituals are the vessels we use to draw up and channel these life-giving waters. The rituals—the practice, the doing—of living are the vessels that draw water from the well. One gift that Judaism offered the world, a deep wellspring of holiness, is **Shabbat**, which the tradition sees as **Heaven on Earth**. Chapter 7 provides us with a glimpse of eternity, for Shabbat is a radically different freedom, a way to be one with the world, the culmination of our weekly journey. All the paths we have traveled in this book lead to Shabbat, **A LIFE OF JOY**.

"You shall draw water joyfully from the springs of salvation" (Isaiah 12:3).

The sources that feed this wellspring are infinite. This book is not about prescribing the right amount of water to draw. "More" is not necessarily better. Too much water can flood the fields and destroy life; or the bucket can be so heavy that we give up trying to lift it. This book *is* about shaping a vessel, lowering it into the well, and drawing up water that will nourish your life.

One of Hebrew's beautiful names for the Divine is Mei-ein HaBrachot—Wellspring of Blessings. This spring is not far away from you; it is very close.

1

צלם אלהים

Tzelem Elohim / A Spark of the Divine

A LIFE ON PURPOSE

You Are Alive for a Reason

Foundational Narrative

God created human beings in the Divine Image, creating them in the image of God, creating them male and female.

Genesis 1:27

Spiritual Expansion

A legend: When God decided to create human beings, the angels were jealous, for angels had not been created in the Divine Image. The angels plotted to hide the Divine Image from human beings. One suggested burying it in the depths of the sea; another in the crag of a jagged mountain. But the most clever of the angels countered: "No! Let's hide the Divine Image within each person. It's the last place they'll ever look."

Torah begins with that story of creation, a desire to give meaning to the universe, to all that is, that life is beautiful and is imbued with purpose: "God saw all that was created and called it very good." That creative force, that surge of energy, still permeates the universe. This reminds me of a vivid memory, walking down my Milgrom family childhood street in Virginia where I grew up. Ours was an old, tree-lined neighborhood, and running down the sidewalk often meant tripping and scraping my knees on jutting blocks of cement. The roots of those old oak trees had pushed the sidewalk up at odd angles. Even with my scraped knee, it was amazing to me that those old roots, in seeking life, could actually move blocks of concrete out of the way. Amazing to realize that the universe pulsates with life, the energy of creation. And inside our hearts, inside life itself, is a powerful force that is the thrust of life. The force of life within us can move blocks of concrete—and clear the way for creativity, for growth, and for love.

Unexpected Encounter

Once, when we were teaching in Palm Springs, a woman we met described a time she was walking down Fifth Avenue in Manhattan. Walking toward her was a beautiful woman, in her words, "beautifully dressed and beautifully coiffed." She stopped the woman and said somewhat apologetically, "I don't usually stop people on the street, but I had to stop and tell you how beautiful you look." The woman said to her, "Actually, I'm going through chemotherapy, and my family told me that I have been looking better than ever, but I didn't believe them until you stopped and told me."

Sometimes we know that we have affected something in an important way—in this case, perhaps a turning point in a woman's recovery from cancer, an affirmation that she is an image of God. It could happen to any of us. Sometimes we are privileged to know the power of a simple act, but most of the time we don't. You don't know what small thing you do might have a huge impact somewhere else. There is no act that need be trivial. We are each alive for a reason. Even what seems meaningless and irrelevant is not without meaning.

The Boy on the Beach

When Yaron (our third child) was in college in upstate New York, he decided he needed to study with a particular professor in New York City. If we would pay for his flights each week (JetBlue was offering flights for $39 each way), he would cram all of his courses into one day, sleep on a friend's couch at college, and fly to New York City each week. But housing in New York City was a major obstacle. Phone calls, internet searches, and newspaper ads yielded no viable results. The whole idea was in serious jeopardy until a friend whose company is in real estate management mentioned to Yaron another possibility: a building that was about to be demolished had one unoccupied apartment, which was now ineligible for renting. If Yaron would be willing to sign a release that he would leave on a day's notice, he could stay there virtually rent free. Yaron went to meet the building super and sign the release on his one-room, empty "palace in the city." The super looked at his name and asked him, "Are you related to David Elcott?" "Yes," Yaron replied. "He's my father."

The man continued:

Many years ago, I took a class with your father in Florida. But to be honest with you, I don't remember anything about the class. What I do remember is that during the break, I took a walk. And I saw him on the beach. He had brought one of his children with him, and he was playing on the beach with his son. I could tell from the way that he was playing with him that nothing else mattered to him at that moment—not the class, not the conference—just this kid. And I said to myself at that time, "If I ever have children, I want to be a father like that to my children."

The super opened his wallet and took out some photographs. "I have three children now," he said to Yaron, "and I think about that scene on the beach every day."

Yaron called David right away. It was a beautiful story—made all the more touching by the fact that it was Yaron who was the little child with David on the beach that day. "I remember that conference," David said. "It felt like the worst thing I ever did. The conference was horrible; no one was in sync with anyone else—it was a total disaster."

Reflecting for a moment, David added, "Sometimes you think the main show is here, when all along, the main show is off to the side." Yaron was seven years old at the time. It took three times that number for Yaron, as a twenty-one-year-old, to intersect with that man's life again, this time across his threshold—and for David to finally learn that the conference hadn't been a disaster after all.

This is one of the important lessons of faith. Under more "normal" circumstances, David would have had the same life-changing impact on this man's life (and subsequently his children's lives) but never known it. So this is faith: to go to sleep at night, thinking perhaps that nothing exceptional happened, that it was just another day—but to know, to believe, that when we act from our center, from a place of focus, of genuine presence, of love, that it somehow affects the world in good ways. And that most of the time, we will never know.

The beginning of faith is to know that beyond the fragmented pieces of our lives there is a whole—a pattern where all the pieces fit together, where we know deep inside that we are each an image of God. You are of infinite value; you deserve to live knowing that you and everyone you meet is an image of God, equal to each other and blessed with Divine-sanctioned uniqueness. There is no one identical to you—even if your sibling is called an identical twin.

There is a remarkable text in the Mishnah, a compilation of rabbinic conversations and debates that took place over the course of a few hundred years at the turn of the millennium. The setting is a courtroom where a man is on trial for his life. The chief justice is questioning a witness who will testify against the accused man. The justice is not gentle and, in an almost threatening tone, tells the witness that a lie that would convict the defendant would be equivalent to murder; the blood of the defendant and any of his potential descendants would be on the head of the witness. These are serious instructions, but the stakes are high. The judge quotes the Bible, explaining that each human being, even one who may be guilty of a heinous crime, is an image of God.

The sages of the Mishnah continue: Why would the Bible open with a story of humanity with the creation of a single human? The Mishnah responds to its own question with three parables. First, to teach that we are each infinitely precious. Because a whole world emerges, as it were, from one human, to save one life is to save the entire world. Second, to teach that we are all equal. Because we all descend from one human, as it were, no one can say, "I am better than you because my ancestor was better than yours." Third, to teach that we are each unique. When a monarch stamps many coins from one seal, each coin is identical. But when the Holy One stamps each of us with the seal of the Divine, as it were, we are each one of us unique.

Angels

It is a custom, when one survives a dangerous or near-death experience, to offer a blessing of thanksgiving at synagogue services. Ari came one Shabbat morning for just that purpose, to offer a blessing and be supported by his community. In our chapel, one cannot simply say a blessing; they must tell a story. So, of course, Ari spoke before reciting the blessing. This is the story he told us.

Ari and his wife, Joan, chose the perfect midweek day to hike in the mountains, quiet and serene. Retirement was made for days like this. They made it up the mountain, enjoyed the spectacular view, and were on their way down when, suddenly, Ari fell to his knees, clutching his chest. Joan tried to pull him up, but alone on the mountain trail, there was nothing she could do, no way she could carry him down. With Ari now lying prone on the ground, her panic rose as she yelled for help, her voice echoing in the forest.

Unbeknownst to Ari and Joan, a group of inner-city high school kids were on a hiking adventure with their counselor. They heard Joan's cries and rushed to the clearing, finding Ari on the ground. Having gone through outdoors training before coming on their hike, these young inner-city teens created a human sling and carried Ari down the mountain while the counselor ran ahead to call 911. The ambulance was waiting and, as Ari was lifted in, Ari grabbed the counselor's hands and said, "You came to me like angels. No words are enough to thank you." The young African American counselor responded to Ari as the students huddled around them listening intently: "I just learned something," he said. "I saw the movie *Schindler's List* about the Holocaust. At the end of the movie, the 1,200 people Schindler saved present him with a simple gold ring, inscribed with the words, 'To save one life is to save the world entire.'"

A movie, a rabbinic text transported over millennia and a lifesaving act meet up in one blazing moment in universal meaning.

The sages of the Mishnah lived in precarious times when human life was worth very little indeed. Rome was all-powerful, a brutally elitist society of entitled citizens and pitiful slaves. Equality was a fantasy left for isolated philosophers. The average life span was but twenty-eight, so many children died young. The empire suppressed dissent, its tentacles reaching over three continents. Yet the rabbis, often themselves under attack, stated unequivocally that all human beings are beloved of and equal in the eyes of God.

The Jewish people nurtured this story of what it means to be a human being through centuries of exile. It was retold, now years ago, by the gentle and deeply moral deputy foreign minister Rabbi Michael Melchior in the opening of Israel's key statement at the United Nation's World Conference against Racism in Durban, South Africa. The conference sadly deteriorated into ugly rancor, but his words spoke powerfully of a different world:

> Why, when the world was created, did God create just one man, Adam, and one woman, Eve? The rabbis answered: so that all

humankind would come from a single union, to teach us that we are all brothers and sisters. This conference was dedicated to that simple proposition. We, all of us, have a common lineage, and are all, irrespective of race, religion, or gender, created in the Divine Image. Indeed, this single idea, unknown to all other ancient civilizations, may be the greatest gift that the Jewish people have given to the world, the recognition of the equality and dignity of every human being.

The sages understood something so profound long before theories of evolution that we humans, along with all life forms, in fact do descend from the same creation. It would be many centuries before the French Enlightenment would offer a declaration stating that all citizens must share equal rights. Two millennia after the Mishnah was codified, the vision so powerfully expressed remains a struggle around the world. Even in my own country, the principle that all Americans are created equal remains a dream.

Yes, we are all minted in the Divine Image, but unlike coins, we are each unique. In this radical theology, the greater the diversity, the more fully we can experience God's Presence in the world. The more we contract and limit human identity, the more God is diminished in the world. At a time when so many demand conformity, undermining each human's uniqueness, we can still work toward this vision of human diversity.

When I, Shira, was in rabbinical school, I had the privilege to study one day with Dr. Abraham Twerski, Hassidic rabbi, scholar, physician, and founder of Gateway Rehabilitation Center, a program on addictions for the Jewish community. I remember how he strode into Hebrew Union College, long black coat, long beard, his tzitzit fringes hanging and earlocks flying behind him—a man unafraid to encounter any human being, at the time violating his own community's restrictions about engaging with Reform rabbis. In one of his many books on addictions and healing, he tells the following story.

The Locket

A young woman was admitted for treatment because of her heroin addiction. All her veins had become obstructed from injecting herself with narcotics. This otherwise pretty woman was a sad sight because of the track marks on her body. She was a nurse and had easy access to drugs. She self-medicated for insomnia and recurring pain. Fearing that the hospital would note the drugs that were missing, she turned to the street and became a heroin addict. She became unable to work, and after running out of money, she sold everything, including herself, for money to buy drugs. Yet she was wearing a beautiful gold locket. Twerski asked her why she had never sold it for heroin. She said that it was her mother's and that she would never part with it. He asked to see it.

When she handed it to him, he picked up a pair of scissors, as if he were about to scratch the locket.

"What are you doing?" she asked in a tone of panic.

"Just scratching this a little bit."

"But that's mine!"

"I know. I will give it back to you."

"But I don't want it all scratched up. It's beautiful, and it's valuable to me."

"You mean that when something has beauty and value, you do not allow it to be marred and ruined?" I asked. Then taking her hands and showing her the bruises and abscesses, I said, "Do you see what this says? These self-inflicted wounds are a loud statement that says, 'I am not beautiful. I have no value.'"[1]

It is so easy for parents, friends, a whole community, to declare with self-righteous indignation: "You are not beautiful. You have no value." What does it mean to validate the uniqueness of a child who is different, who marches to a different drummer? It is a difficult task, as we know, to parent each child in ways that affirm their uniqueness and infinite value while also strengthening their capacity to become the person they can be. And what does it mean for a community, a society, to treasure the uniqueness of each member, not allowing the expectations and prejudices of past generations to destroy the spirit, the unique image of God with which each person has been blessed?

For us, too, to become the person we were meant to be, the fullness of being an image of God, to initiate a process of self-transformation, we need to locate a baseline of self-love. Sometimes when we don't believe it, asserting that we are worthy, that we are deserving of love, is an act of faith. Knowing ourselves as worthy, we can initiate a path of growth and transformation.

We do not believe in a static universe. "It's just the way it is" is not good enough. We remember a billboard on the West Side Highway, in the years when the tobacco industry was still trying to maintain its American market. It showed a beautiful woman and a pack of cigarettes with the words: "There is no alternative but being yourself." There is an alternative: "Becoming yourself." Becoming is about growing and changing. Becoming is about giving birth to yourself. Giving birth to oneself, becoming and changing, brings vulnerability and risk.

This is illustrated brilliantly by the life of the lobster. A lobster is encased in a hard shell, and it grows until it reaches the outside limits of the shell. It then finds a secluded shelter and sheds its shell and slowly grows a new one. It does this several times until it reaches its full growth. Each time the lobster sheds its shell, it becomes open and vulnerable. In order to grow, the lobster must shed its defenses. Change and transformation involve taking enormous risks.

Delancey Street

Many years ago, when our children were still small, we spent a summer driving cross-country. Among the sites we visited was a place called Delancey Street. We will tell you that our kids ranked this place up there along with the Grand Canyon. Delancey Street, located in San Francisco, is a facility dedicated to the rehabilitation of men and women convicted of felonies. This facility, as it turned out, was stunning: courtyards, fountains, balconies overflowing with flowers, views of the San Francisco Bay, and men and women walking around dressed in suits and dresses. "Every person you will meet," we were told, "has been incarcerated in maximum security."

These well-dressed, kindly-spoken people were each "doing time" in Delancey Street. But there were no prison wardens, no guards, no locks on the doors or gates, no professionals. Doing time in Delancey Street is much more demanding and much harder than doing time in prison, they say. But for those who make it through three years, and there have been more than ten thousand of them, there is virtually no return to crime.

Though not a religious institution, Delancey Street is dedicated to one of the most profoundly religious beliefs, the possibility of profound change and personal transformation. The possibility of change is a foundational Jewish belief. We do not believe in original sin, the notion that every human embryo is stigmatized by an original, involuntary sin, like DNA, inherited from conception. Our sins are not inherited; they are of our own doing, and we are responsible for and capable of changing our lives.

When a resident of Delancey Street is deemed by their peers to be ready, he or she is brought to a room at the top of the Delancey Street complex, a room they have dubbed "the Vatican." For three days, seventy-two hours, the resident is not allowed to leave this room; he is provided with food and water and a bathroom, but is kept awake—as peers question him about his life, or give her the chance to face the ghosts in her closet—unresolved guilt and still-hidden truths. For they understand that personal transformation will not succeed without this process of the deepest introspection and confession. The courage to become ourselves requires openness and risk.

The gentleman who took us around Delancey Street explained that one of the things that came out during his grueling days in this "Vatican" room was that years earlier, while he had been in prison for murder, his own mother had died. He told his peers that he never had the chance to say good-bye, never had the chance to make amends. The next thing he knew, his fellow residents were walking into the room with a coffin. "If this were your mother," they said to him, "what would you say to her?" And this once-hardened criminal described to us how he had wept, and talked, and wept. And unburdened his heart. Genuine transformation causes more change, and it ripples. His open heart opened ours. None of us will forget that day.

Tzelem Elohim—the Divine Image. This foundational belief that we are each created with a spark of the Divine means that we are each infinitely precious, each unique. It means that we are equally obligated to bring our own blessing to the world. No one can do our part but we ourselves; our actions have cosmic significance. The poetic brushstrokes of Genesis painted a daring vision, one in which every human is created in the Divine Image, unique and irreplaceable. We still must work hard to see that vision fully realized.

2

ברית

Brit / Covenant

A LIFE OF CONNECTION

Learning to Love

Foundational Narrative

It is not good for a human to be alone.

Genesis 2:18

I bore you on eagles' wings and brought you to Me. Now then, if you will obey me faithfully and keep My covenant, you shall be My treasure. Indeed, all the earth is Mine, but you shall be to Me a kingdom of priests and a holy nation.

Exodus 19:4–6

Spiritual Expansion

Everyone has experienced moments of wonder and amazement—as small as a pattern on a leaf, an unexpected gesture of kindness, a heart-stopping sunset, an exquisite butterfly, a full moon being birthed from the landscape—moments we might describe as spiritual, or awe-inspiring, even transcendent. "Religion is not made of these moments; religion is the means of making these moments part of your life rather than merely radical intrusions."[1]

A spiritual practice is a doing—a discipline—that brings wonder and amazement, joy and gratitude, into everyday moments of life.

Spiritual Expansion

Rachel Naomi Remen describes one of her earliest childhood memories with her grandfather. He brought her a gift of a paper cup. Looking inside, she was somewhat dismayed to find that it was filled with dirt. "Put some water in it every day," he told her, "and something extraordinary may happen." Every day, she filled her little teapot with water and put some water in the cup. One week—nothing. A second week—nothing. It was so hard to keep up this practice. One day, two tiny green leaves appeared. She couldn't wait to tell her grandfather.

> Carefully he explained to me that life is everywhere, hidden in the most ordinary and unlikely places. I was delighted. "And all it needs is water, Grandpa?" I asked him. Gently he touched me on the top of my head. "No, Neshume-le," he said. "All it needs is your faithfulness."[2]

A mature relationship doesn't begin until after disappointment.
Michael Vincent Miller

Holy Obligation (Mitzvah)

Our American culture was founded on the principle of personal autonomy. We center our lives on self-sufficiency, wealth accumulation, and self-fulfillment. How are we doing? On February 3, 2025, a broad and politically diverse group of scholars issued a report card for America. The State of the Union Project's mission states that it "is a comprehensive and objective national progress report assessing how we are doing as a nation. Our report represents a broad consensus of leading experts and a cross-section of everyday Americans from across the political spectrum." Its report card: America has the world's second-largest economy, behind only China. At the same time, by many other measures of well-being—especially health and happiness—America ranks worse than most other wealthy countries and continues to fall further and further behind.

We have

> the lowest life expectancy of any rich country, which was not true for most of the 20th century. The U.S. has the highest murder rate of any rich country and the world's highest rate of fatal drug overdoses. It also has one of the lowest rates of trust in the federal government and among the highest rates of youth depression and single-parent families. When Americans are asked how satisfied they are with their own lives, the U.S. ranks lower than it did three decades ago.

The most common theme that emerged from all the researchers was that of social isolation.[3]

And it's not just this national progress report. Research studies, books, and articles across disciplines as far ranging as sociology and ecology, from *Bowling Alone* to *Braiding Sweetgrass*, have arrived at the same conclusion: happiness, health, and thriving increase with interdependence and reliance on one another and decrease with separateness, competition, and self-reliance.

It is not good for human beings to be alone (Genesis 2:8).

We don't do well without committed relationships—not as human beings and not as a society. Relationship and obligation go hand in hand. We understand that a relationship that does not have any claims on us is not a serious relationship. Any worthwhile relationship—a child, a spouse, a close friend—makes claims on us and engenders obligation. This view is reflected in ancient Jewish sources.

The sages of the Talmud ask and then respond:

> Q: Who does a greater act—the one who is commanded/obligated to do it or the one who chooses to do it?
> A: Greater is one who is commanded and acts than the one who is not commanded and does so voluntarily.
>
> Kiddushin 31a

The answer of the sages is counterintuitive. Everything we have been taught in our own culture would bring us to answer differently: obviously, the one who of their own free will chooses to do something, this is the higher deed. Indeed, "obligation" has gotten a bad rap over the past decades. Perhaps this illustration provided by David in his book *A Sacred Journey* will help:

> A young single woman walks through a park and sees two children, a brother and a sister, fighting. She kneels down and sweetly separates the children, resolving their conflict with a few words. Undoubtedly, it is a virtuous act, a good deed. The same two

children then return home, where an older brother is cramming for a college exam. Actually, he has just taken a break to repair a leaking faucet and is now throwing some leftovers together for dinner with his siblings. Exhausted from a grueling week of study, he hears the two fighting—for the fifth time that day. He tries to ignore the screaming, feels his temper rising. Instead of exploding, however, he takes a deep breath, kneels down (not so sweetly) to separate the kids, resolving their conflict with a few words.

The contrasting scenes can shed light on what the sages so valued in the person who lives with a sense of relationship that commands obligation. The voluntary actions of the young woman in the park are virtuous but undependable. But the brother acts out of a deep sense of relationship and obligation, which is what the sages valued so highly. Their behaviors are covenantal, motivated by love and long-term commitment—a sparse commodity in our age. Sacredness is not merely a product of a particular activity at a particular moment, but the willingness to commit one's whole life to a web of relationships, obligations and purpose.[4]

Generosity, free will, loving—these are all wonderful. But they don't always come naturally. The heart needs help; the heart needs to be shaped and strengthened. Imagine the all-too-familiar scene of a young child opening birthday presents—your niece or nephew, your child or grandchild. As the wrapping paper comes off, you see right away that the child already has one of these, or that the gift is not something the child would want. The child has been taught to express their true feelings—but at this moment, we are praying that the child will not express their feelings! What are we hoping for? We are hoping that the child will rise to the challenge of the moment and say "thank you." We are not requiring that the child deny their thoughts or feelings ("If this person really knew me, they wouldn't have gotten me this present"); we are hoping and expecting that the child will be thinking of and prioritizing the feelings of the one who gave the present. How do we bring a child to this awareness of the other? How many times do we say to the child, "And what do you say? Say thank you." How many thousands of times? The doing—the regular doing—the ritualized obligation to say "thank you" gradually shapes a heart of awareness, thoughtfulness, and gratitude.

And, besides, loving is hard.
Loving takes commitment. Faithfulness.

For some religious traditions, their foundational stories reflect unwavering faith and clear and certain dogma. The early narratives of the emerging Israelite people are different. If anything, the through line of these stories is doubt and a struggle with faithfulness. Yes, the Torah relates that God took the Israelites out of Egypt with a mighty hand and an outstretched arm. "I bore you on eagles' wings," God said, "and brought you to Me" (Exodus 19:4). "Will you be a kingdom of priests and a holy nation; will you be faithful to me?" God had asked then. "Yes, yes, we will. We do," the Israelites had said. And they surely meant it.

But it was so hard to hold that faith together. The Torah tells us the honeymoon lasted for only three days. The desert, it seems, wasn't the best choice to engender faithfulness. Three days later, the people were tired and thirsty and disgruntled. "Why did we ever get into this relationship? Are there not enough graves in Egypt," they cried to Moses, "that you brought us to this wilderness to die?" Ten plagues—the crossing of the sea—all these narratives of spectacular moments. Apparently one gigantic miracle does no more to nurture faith than one big meal does to end hunger.

Nurturing faith and nurturing loving have a lot in common.

Most of us have been brought up to believe that loving comes naturally—that there isn't much that needs to be, or can be, learned about love. But for many of us, loving is something we learn to do our whole lives—with friends who change, with parents who mature, and even with our children, as they grow through different stages, challenging what we have taught them, exerting their independence.

When we think of the challenges of faithfulness in a relationship, it is often marriage that comes to mind first. However, in today's world, nearly half of all adult Americans have chosen not to be in a relationship of marriage at all. That does not release us from the urgency to create and sustain faithful and loving relationships in our lives. There are many other ways. Each of us needs to nurture faithful and committed relationships.

For many of us, the challenge of loving becomes most intense with our life partner. We grow up thinking: if only I would meet the right person, then love's first kiss will sweep me off my feet and bring me happiness ever after. "Of all the misconceptions about love, the most powerful and pervasive is the belief that 'falling in love' is love…. No matter with whom we fall in love, we sooner or later fall out of love if the relationship continues long enough."[5] Here's the important piece. The end of falling in love is where the work of real loving can begin. It's where many of us give up.

"Romantic love is beautiful, but no matter how full the moon that first night, no matter how many willows are weeping and birds singing your song, you can't build years of relationship on that lovely, fragile foundation alone. Everything I've learned from my work with people disappointed in love," writes Dr. Michael Vincent Miller, "points to this conclusion: A mature relationship doesn't begin until after disappointment."[6]

More and more of us are disappointed with love. We might seek intensity in sexual encounters. We give up on our relationships—check out emotionally—or end them. Or rather than commit to relationship at all, we'll try the glamour of the swinging life—another woman, another man. We hope that the next affair will bring lasting happiness.

It turns out that our brains are wired against us in this endeavor of finding happiness and pleasure in what is steady and familiar. It turns out that the job of our brains is to regulate us and to normalize sensory input. So, for example, stepping into a room that is brightly or dimly lit, our brain instructs our eyes to adjust to the different levels of illumination. The same is true of all other kinds of sensory input. Returning home from a week of camping, that first hot shower feels like heaven on earth. But a week later, we don't even notice it. Our brains are not trying to keep us happy; our brains are trying to regulate us. We don't realize how quickly we will adapt to a pleasurable sensation and make it the background of our lives. When any extraordinary event happens to us, we make it ordinary. And through becoming ordinary, we lose our pleasure.

According to research, it's not just that we lose our pleasure—making beautiful and new things ordinary, to be expected and taken for granted. It's that we also can't seem to remember that we will do this again and again. So we really think that the next thing will make us happier—the newer car, the next upgrade, the other woman or the next man.

So is it all about biology?

Though some aspects of being human are governed by our biology, the development of character is not. Character is not something we are born with; character is something we develop. Loving and fidelity are qualities of character.

The end of falling in love is where the work of real loving can begin. Real loving gives us the unparalleled chance to grow—and this is for husbands and wives, life partners, parents with their children, children with their parents, siblings with each other, and friends with friends. No full relationship can grow without commitment. Children cannot grow up to spiritual and emotional maturity under the specter of abandonment, and couples cannot work to resolve the issues of their relationship if they fear that honest sharing will destroy their relationship.

Clearly, not all relationships can be repaired. In the complicated world of human relationships, we know that sometimes there are limits to our loving. There are abusive relationships—there are abusive parents, abusive partners, and abusive friends. That should not stop us from believing that love is possible. Learning to love is among the most extraordinary things that human beings can do. Loving requires the nurturing of faithfulness. My faithfulness as a person does not depend on others; I cannot blame anyone else if I am or am not faithful. My faithfulness is a quality that I nurture myself.

The Northern Lights

For as long as I can remember, I have been fascinated by the northern lights—the aurora borealis. What an unbelievable sight that must be—magnificent, awe-inspiring curtains of light in purples, blues, and greens—spread out like magic across the sky. I said to David that all I wanted for my fiftieth birthday was to see the northern lights. So we went to Alaska so that I could chase after them. But I learned that you can chase after them, but that doesn't mean you're going to see them. Even when it is aurora season, they do not appear on command. After five days, I took a photograph of the sign marking Northern Lights Boulevard—and we boarded the plane for home. But I wasn't unhappy. It was good to learn that life is not something we are entitled to—it is always a gift of grace, undeserved.

Returning from Israel for my father's eightieth birthday via London, two years later, the pilot's voice came over the loudspeaker explaining that significant storm activity over the Atlantic Ocean had forced a rerouting of the plane north toward the Arctic Circle, where we would then head west for our return to the States. Passengers aboard the plane groaned, knowing this would delay our return. I sat up in my seat. It was winter—and nighttime—and we were heading toward the Arctic Circle. And as people slept, I sat in my seat and watched the lights. They started slowly—an aura of green at the edge of the horizon—and they grew into columns and walls of white light. The direct experience, the infinity of brilliant changing patterns, has faded. But I remember the curtains—the curtains of light—hanging from the top of the heavens, blowing across the sky in some invisible wind, fringed with red. I fell onto the floor (and there isn't a lot of space between the seat and the tray table) and wept—in gratitude and in prayer.

Centuries ago, the Kabbalists of Safed wrote a meditation as an introduction to putting on the prayer shawl, the tallit. Their meditation, their *kavanna*, draws from the book of Psalms. It reads like this: "*Barchi nafshi et adonai*—Bless the Eternal, O my soul. You wrap yourself in light as with a garment; You stretch out the heavens like a curtain" (Psalm 104)—and then you swing the tallit around your shoulders and wrap yourself. And I vowed at that moment, kneeling on the floor of the plane, that I would wrap myself in the tallit every morning, and I would recall this gift of life and wonder.

I learned and understood something that I had not understood before, and that is the experience of God's faithfulness. I learned that God is faithful, that is, that the potential for wonder is there all the time. And I learned that I had been the one who hadn't been faithful. At some point I realized that I had stopped putting on the tallit. I had stopped feeling the sense of obligation every morning to give thanks for the gifts of my life, for life itself. We owe a huge debt of gratitude for the gift of our lives, and feeling the obligation to acknowledge it helps shape a religious—a spiritual—soul. By nurturing our faithfulness, it also brings us back to a sense of wonder.

Even the wonder embedded in otherwise ordinary things.

If you wander into our kitchen, you might notice a meditation written by the Vietnamese Buddhist monk Thich Nhat Hanh that we keep above the kitchen sink. He suggests that we should wash dishes as if we are bathing the baby Buddha—that if you can't wait to finish the dishes so you can have a cup of tea, you won't enjoy either washing the dishes, or the cup of tea. It's a meditation on the moment—and on living now. It's a reminder that happiness, like loving, cannot be deferred; happiness is a decision for this moment, for now. Happiness is a product of attention, faithful attention.

Experiencing God's Presence now—in this moment—challenges us in the same way a commitment to a loved one does. Faith and fidelity. It is easy to be disappointed, forgetting God's faithfulness—what have you done for me lately?—and it is easy to be disappointed with love. Surely that was the problem of the Israelites. In the dream imagery of the Torah, the signs and wonders, the pillar of fire and the pillar of cloud, the splitting of the sea, and God's redemptive Presence everywhere, and all it took was three days of serious troubles, and—Where is God now? But we don't have to be stuck there, in a place disconnected from God or from the forces of loving. Rabbi David Wolpe has noted that from a distance, looking at a rower on a lake, it looks like the shore is moving closer and closer to the boat. But of course it is the movement of the rower that brings him closer; the shore is always there and waiting.

Fidelity. Fidelity is a quality of character. We can be a faithful friend, a faithful spouse, a faithful parent. We also work to be faithful to ourselves, to the values that we hold dear. Sometimes these fidelities are in conflict; sometimes being faithful to myself may mean ending a relationship. We know of no formula for figuring out the balance of all these things. But cultivating the quality of fidelity—in the different ways that it can manifest—is a good thing. Fidelity is a beautiful thing. As Will Durant said about his marriage to his Ariel to whom he was married more than sixty years, "The love we have in our youth is superficial compared to that an old man has for his old wife."

Several years ago, the *Jewish Week* asked couples married forty years or more to share their secrets on keeping their marriage blissful. One man said: "Ethel and I have been married 47 years and two secrets have kept our marriage going. Since we were first married, we have made it a practice to go out twice a week for a romantic dinner with candlelight, champagne and dancing. Ethel goes out on Tuesdays and I go out on Fridays."

Cultivating fidelity and commitment isn't easy, and a sense of humor and cutting everyone lots of slack certainly help.

"Faithful" is to commit to something larger than myself, something beyond how I feel at this or that moment. There are many ways to cultivate faithfulness. In the religious vocabulary of Judaism, "faithful" translates as "mitzvah"—something you do out of a sense of commitment. Shabbat is such a faithful mitzvah.

Week in, week out, ready or not, here it is. Shabbat means that a week won't go by without our telling the people we love the most that life wouldn't be what it is without them. Shabbat means that we won't accept invitations to go out with another couple, leaving members of the family at home. Shabbat means regular, dependable time when our children can count on their parents being home—when parents can count on their children being home.

In our life, Shabbat has meant holding our children—each child—blessing them and kissing them, cultivating faithfulness. Every Shabbat of our marriage, at the Friday evening Shabbat table, David has held me and sung to me in the words of our tradition. There were times, particularly in our early years, when we were so tired and hassled, and the days were so busy and crazy, that we didn't take the time to tell each other that we loved one another. And there were weeks that I felt ignored—and that David's work, or the children's needs, were more important to him than me. And when he held me on Friday night and sang to me, I would think to myself, "Why is he holding me and singing to me? Everything else in his life is more important than me: his kids, his colleagues, his work." And what I would find was that in his holding me, I would remember our love; I would remember the loving person that I wanted to be. And if our tradition didn't have Friday night? If those words were not a faithful commitment—a mitzvah of our Shabbat? Would David tell me on Friday night—each Friday night—that he loved me? Even if he were angry? Even if he too felt ignored? Even if he didn't feel like it?

Love is critical, but faithfulness brings us back when love falters. A life of mitzvah—of commitment—helps to nurture faithfulness. Even when we do not feel like it—when we are exhausted at the end of a week—it brings us back to what is most important, and it brings us back to ourselves. Coming back is a quality of faithfulness. Most of us are not "faithful" all the time; in small ways and large, we err, we pull away, we shut down. But commitment and faithfulness bring us back.

When you wonder where God is in your life, remember your joys and your losses and your reasons for gratitude. God is present in all of it—hidden in these and in all the ordinary moments of our lives—waiting to be encountered in a moment of amazement, in moments of openness and noticing and wonder. You are capable of wonder and amazement and loving. Wonder and connection and loving and hope are always there. God is faithful—and waiting. Waiting only for our faithfulness.

Spiritual Practice / Ritual

Our daughter Talia meets her best friend every Thursday morning—rain or shine—for a morning walk. They put their kids on the bus to school and spend an hour walking together. We were moved by this simple and powerful practice. You can find and create your own ritual.

Key ingredients:

- Faithfulness. Stick to it.
- Regularity. Same time; predictable.
- Enduring. It's not a one-time event. You're in it for the long haul.
- Sustainable. Make it something you can do.

The more you stay with it, the more it will give to you and bless you.

3

תשובה

Teshuva / Healing and Return

A LIFE OF INNER GROWTH

The Courage to Become You

Foundational Narrative

You are Healer of shattered hearts and Binder of our wounds.

Psalm 147:3

Spiritual Expansion

The Torah tells us that as Moses descended from Mount Sinai with the tablets in his hands, on seeing the Israelites in wild idolatrous worship around a golden calf, Moses—whether in anger or despair—hurled the tablets to the ground, shattering them to pieces.

Moses seeks reconciliation on behalf of his people. God gives the Israelites a second chance—and Moses is summoned to the mountaintop to carve a new set.

Generations later, the sages of the Talmud wondered what could have happened to the broken pieces of the first set. The Talmud answers in five words:

Luchot v'shivrei luchot munachim ba-aron.
The whole tablets and the shattered tablets rest in the ark.

Talmud Bava Batra 14b

A deeply insightful Hassidic sage, the Kotzker Rebbe, added: "There is nothing as whole as a broken heart."

There is a place within us for the broken pieces of our lives; they, too, are holy. Our wholeness and our brokenness together make us complete.

The Crystal Bowl

In 1920, our children's great-grandmother received a beautiful crystal punch bowl as a wedding gift. It was a one-of-a-kind, hand-cut piece, later valued at $10,000. We tell you this so you should know that it wasn't just any punch bowl. Mutti, like her family for the preceding five centuries, lived in Germany. By the late 1930s, the grip of Nazi rule began to tighten around Mutti's life. But Mutti was reluctant to leave her country and her home. For what a home it was. Mutti had overseen the construction of this beautiful, four-story home.

One day in November 1938, Mutti's older daughter, Ruth, then a teenager, had an uneasy premonition. She convinced her parents and her younger sister to leave the house. They were hidden in the home of faithful Christian friends. Before she herself left, she pushed a large armoire into the end of a stair landing, creating behind it a false closet. She hid there the two most precious things for her and her family—her personal diary and the crystal bowl. The date was November 9, 1938.

That night was Kristallnacht, the Night of Broken Glass, as organized riots of Nazi Germans destroyed synagogues and Jewish-owned businesses all over Germany. When the rioting subsided by the morning of the tenth, Ruth would still not let her family return home. The uneasy feeling hadn't left her. And indeed, it was the following night that their home was destroyed.

Ruth returned home alone on the third morning, the fate of their home still unknown. As Ruth rounded the corner of their street on her bicycle, she saw from a distance the front door of their home lying in the middle of the street. As she got closer, she could see water pouring out of the open doorway. The Nazis had stopped up all the drains and turned on the faucets. As she slowly climbed the stairs, she saw the family portraits that lined the staircase slashed—knives pierced through the eyes and hearts of generations of her family. But they hadn't found her diary or the crystal bowl.

The crystal bowl followed Mutti and her family on their escape route, from Germany, to England, to Chicago, and finally to Los Angeles. When Mutti died in 1990, the crystal bowl passed to her first grandchild, Diane, who lives in Northridge. Diane had always loved the bowl and treasured it not as her own; she knew that it was in her safekeeping to preserve for all of Mutti's generations still to come.

Four years later, an earthquake hit Los Angeles, centered in Northridge. David, in a quirk of fate, heard about the earthquake as it was happening and got a call through to his sister before all the phone lines went down. He could hear the pictures falling down from the walls, windows shattering, glass flying. It was like another Kristallnacht. And Diane was hysterical: "Mutti's bowl! Mutti's bowl!" was all she could scream. David kept saying, "You're all alright. Nothing else matters." But Mutti's bowl had fallen and broken into a hundred pieces, and Diane was inconsolable.

The city of Los Angeles began to clean up; daily, trucks circled through neighborhoods picking up the huge piles of debris stacked outside the homes. But Diane kept the pieces of the crystal bowl. One night she had a dream and awoke knowing what she needed to do. On her own, she commissioned an artist friend to make a sculpture of Mutti. After studying photographs and videos, the artist molded a clay form of Mutti, and then poured fourteen bronze statues, one for each of Mutti's children, grandchildren, and great-grandchildren. When they were finished, Diane presented them to her family. Mutti is seated on a stool, with her hands in her lap. And in each statue, placed in her hands, is a piece of the crystal bowl.

Just because something breaks and shatters into pieces doesn't mean that it's over. Part of healing our lives is the faith that we are part of something bigger. Broken dreams, failures, disappointments, struggles, pain and suffering. We can take the broken pieces of our lives and create from them something new. A legacy of love that will be for the generations.

Spiritual Expansion

When our heart breaks.

> Love the Eternal with all your heart, with all your soul and with all your might.
> These words which I command you this day shall be upon your heart.
>
> Deuteronomy 6:5–6

The Kotzker Rebbe: How odd is that? Place these words *on* your heart? Why wouldn't the Torah have written *in* your heart? Because, he answered, sometimes your heart is hardened and nothing can get in. So place these words on your heart, and sometime, when your heart cracks open, in a time of heartbreak, the words will be lying there, and they will fall in.

ON PRAYER

Pain and joy rub up at the same edge; gratitude and loss; we sit at the great moments of our lives or perhaps that of our children or others we care about—at weddings and baby namings, graduations, and anniversaries—and we cry, we say, for joy. And it is joy. But it is also awareness of the preciousness of it all; it is so fragile and so deep and so wonderful and so vulnerable all at the same time.

Many years ago, after Diane and her husband, Jeff, dropped off their first child at college, they had to pull off the highway because they were crying so hard. And four years later, when he graduated and moved back home, they cried even harder. Ends and beginnings—they are all wrapped up together. And our hearts sing for the wonder of it all, for the wonder and gift of being alive. This is the gratitude that prayer can express—however we do it, in whatever language or religious setting.

The Hebrew word for "blessing"—*bracha*—comes from the word *berech*, meaning "knee." There is something at the heart of prayer that can bring us to our knees. The time I saw the northern lights from a plane—a sky moving with white curtains of light fringed with red—there was nothing to do but drop to my knees—and pray. I don't remember that I said anything; it was just dropping to my knees and praying. There are also times when we feel we have run out of possibilities, when we hit rock bottom, or when we know we need more help, more wisdom, more power than we can muster ourselves. And then, too, we drop to our knees. We have done that, too.

It is a custom in so many faith traditions to kneel or prostrate ourselves. Many churches we have visited have padded knee rests. Muslims prostrate themselves, performing *sujud* twice toward the end of each *raka'ah*, each section of prayer. Buddhists bow in humility and surrender, a reverent moment of deep respect toward the Buddha and his teachings. While Jews bend their knees and bow in prayer daily, on Yom Kippur it is the Jewish custom to prostrate oneself to acknowledge God's grace. It is not the prayer of asking God to do anything. It is acknowledging how much we depend on a world so much bigger than we are.

On a beautiful Shabbat morning years ago, we were in the chapel when a gift was being announced to the group. It was a generous contribution of $10,000 to airlift Ethiopian Jews from the terrors they faced. The note read that this generous gift had been issued in honor of the worshippers in that Shabbat morning group, and though it wasn't for us, it clearly honored us and in some indirect way benefited us. Though anonymous giving isn't always the best or preferred kind of giving, this gift was anonymous. The giver or givers had protected their anonymity by issuing a banker's check—and though we had no idea who they were, we had the feeling that morning that they were present. In a flash of rare spiritual insight, it became clear: "If only we could live our lives this way, knowing that our life is a gift, and that we stand in the Presence of the Unnamed Giver."

We fall to our knees because it is all a gift. We are not entitled to life; we did nothing to deserve it. It is a gift of love. And yes, we are loved.

Pregnant at Forty-Two

Dr. Abraham Twerski recounts how, at an Al-Anon meeting, Nora narrated the pain of her ordeal. She had dealt with her husband's alcoholism for many years, followed by the many blessings they enjoyed in the years of their sobriety. The one major disappointment in her life had been that she could not get pregnant. Nevertheless, they made peace with their fate and adopted two children.

In what seemed a miracle of God's blessing, Nora became pregnant at forty-two, only to explode in anger and pain when she held in her arms a baby with Down syndrome. She prayed every night for God to change him. After months of prayer, she said, the true miracle did occur. "God answered our prayer and changed us. And I understood that if I love this child with all his defects, then I know for certain that God can love me even with all my defects."[1]

For some of us, those into whose arms we were born, or with whom we have shared our life, have not loved us—they weren't able, or they didn't know how, or they didn't want to. And the ache of that emptiness is deep. But love is deeper. You are made of love—and you can find it again. Pain and joy both bring us back to this awareness.

Perhaps many of you already know what we came to know: when we pray the prayer of the heart, our heart connects to the heart of the universe. We have found that when we drop to our knees and acknowledge, "I need help. I need help to become the person I want to be," we find that we are not alone. In prayer, the very act of reaching out creates the connection.

The Cello

When I was a child in Virginia, my cello teacher demonstrated to me the way that harmonic sounds work. He took the bow of the cello and pulled it back and forth across the G string—and as the sound filled the room, the other strings, one by one, began to vibrate. Perhaps this is true for prayer. Like everything that exists, our spirit, our soul, is made of the stuff of the universe. When we let our souls sing, the God within us vibrates with the love and spirit of the universe. This is a gift worth pursuing, in whatever language and tradition—or no words at all—in song, in dance, in meditation, in moments of sublime joy or despair. Even in moments when we feel nothing at all. When we pray, we can move past our angers and our fears and our judgment of ourselves and others; we find that even deeper than darkness and anger is forgiveness—the prayer of the heart connects us to what is deepest within: compassion and gratitude and joy.

Reb Nachman of Bratislav, a holy man wracked by doubt and shame, wrote his heartfelt prayer of longing to the God of his soul.

Grant me the ability to be alone;
may it be my custom to go outdoors each day among the trees
and grass—among all growing things and there may I be alone,
and enter into prayer,
to talk with the One to whom I belong.
May I express there everything in my heart,
and may all the foliage of the field—all grasses, trees, and
plants—awake at my coming,
to send the powers of their life into the words of my prayer
so that my prayer and speech are made whole through the life
and spirit of all growing things,
which are made as one by their transcendent Source.
May I then pour out the words of my heart before your
Presence like water, O Eternal, and lift up my hands to You in
worship, on my behalf, and that of my children!

Spiritual Practice / Ritual

Times of serious illness are also liminal moments that call out for prayer. Different religious traditions have profoundly different ideas of God's direction or intervention in our lives. This prayer for healing is not a petition. It reinforces a theology that God is present within us—and that when people reach out to heal, God is present between us. Whatever the outcome of illness, the spiritual longing expressed in this prayer remains true and valid: our prayer and the caring of others connect us to the heart of life. This prayer of the heart can be recited alone for oneself, or shared when visiting a patient.

A Prayer for Healing

> In my illness, I turn to You, for I am Your creation.
> Your strength and courage are in my spirit
> And Your powers of healing are within my body.
> In my illness I have learned what is great and what is small.
> I know how dependent I am upon You.
> My own pain and anxiety have been my teachers.
> May I never forget this precious knowledge
> when I am well again.
> Bless the agents of Your healing, the physicians and the nurses,
> my community of friends and family
> with wisdom and patience.
> Their presence and dedication connect me to life itself
> and to You.
> Blessed are You, the faithful and merciful Healer. Amen.

The places of brokenness within us can also become the places of healing. But often, before they become a place of healing, they can be places of shame.

ON SHAME AND FORGIVENESS

Phyllis and Orlando Rodriguez's son, Greg, was killed on September 11, 2001, one of three thousand who perished in the attack on the World Trade Center. Within the week, a copy of a letter they wrote ended up in my synagogue inbox.

> ### Not in Our Son's Name
> Our son Greg is among the many missing from the World Trade Center attack. Since we first heard the news, we have shared

moments of grief, comfort, hope, despair, fond memories with his wife, the two families, our friends and neighbors, his loving colleagues at Cantor Fitzgerald/eSpeed, and all the grieving families that daily meet at the Pierre Hotel.

We see the hurt and anger reflected among everybody we meet. We cannot pay attention to the daily flow of news about this disaster. But we read enough of the news to sense that our government is heading in the direction of violent revenge, with the prospect of sons, daughters, parents, friends in distant lands dying, suffering, and nursing further grievances against us. It is not the way to go. It will not avenge our son's death. Not in our son's name.

Our son died a victim of an inhuman ideology. Our actions should not serve the same purpose. Let us grieve. Let us reflect and pray. Let us think about a rational response that brings real peace and justice to our world. But let us not as a nation add to the inhumanity of our times.

September 2001

I kept this letter in the pocket of my Friday night prayer book for six years, not knowing how or when I would use it. It took me six years to learn that Phyllis Rodriguez was a Jewish woman and that she lived in White Plains.

The following year, in 2002, Phyllis met Aicha el-Wafi, whose son Zacarias Moussaoui had been charged with conspiracy in connection with the attacks. Aicha had traveled from France to New York for a private meeting with families who lost loved ones in the terrorist attacks.

PHYLLIS (remembering that terrible day of 9/11): I was listening to a phone message from Greg saying there had been a terrible accident at the World Trade Center. I didn't know which tower he worked in, but when I saw on television the second plane crash into the second tower, I knew it was no accident. I rang family and friends and said: "He called; he's OK." I couldn't take it in until it was officially announced the following evening that he had perished along with three thousand others. When Greg was killed, I thought, I will never forgive the people who murdered my son.

AICHA: On September 13, 2001, I was in bed, and my daughter called me to tell me that Zacarias was on television. I couldn't recognize my son—the picture was horrible. I knelt down in front of the TV and yelled, "It's not true, it's not my son, it's not possible."

While I knew my son was not directly responsible for the attacks, extremist thinking like his had created a climate of hate. When I thought of the people who died and of their families, I knew my suffering was not the same and I wanted to present my condolences and apologize.

The evening before meeting the families, I was so nervous I couldn't sleep, but the French human rights interpreter I was with encouraged me by telling me I was doing the right thing. The next morning, we took the subway, and my heart was beating double time as I walked down the hallway. Then I entered the room where all these family members were waiting, and my eyes landed on Phyllis—something like a magnet drew me to her. We fell into each other's arms and cried for a long time. I felt her heart beating as fast as mine. It was painful and wonderful at the same time.

Although I am not responsible for the choices my son has made as an adult, I still feel guilty because I gave birth to him. I so wish that Zacarias hadn't gotten involved with al-Qaida, but he fell into the hands of crooks. In Bin Laden, he was looking for a father figure because his own father was violent with him and then abandoned us. I feel anger, love, and compassion for Zacarias. A part of me is dead, buried with my son who will have to spend the rest of his life in jail.[2]

Phyllis and Aicha have since partnered in an organization called the Forgiveness Project. Victims and persecutors—they and their family members—from South Africa, Romania, Israel, Palestine, Northern Ireland, England, and America, have joined together to open up conversation around forgiveness and revenge, weakness and strength, justice and morality. Theirs are stories of people who have survived tragedy, who have lived through atrocity, and who have it in themselves to talk about forgiveness.

Every religious tradition addresses the need for repentance and forgiveness. All human beings err; all of us are in need of forgiveness. In Jewish tradition, the new year begins with a process of self-reflection and repentance. We believe that change is possible, that we are not stuck in the destructive behaviors of the past; we believe that we can begin anew. This process of change, *teshuva*, begins on the new year and continues through ten days of repentance—*aseret y'mei teshuva*—culminating in the twenty-four-hour fast of Yom Kippur.

The process of *teshuva*, repentance, begins with the self. Two thousand years ago, two great rabbis, Rabbi Akiva and Rabbi Ben Azzai, debated the question of what is the most important verse in the Torah. Akiva, in an oft-quoted statement, said the most important verse in the Torah is "Love your neighbor as yourself." Ben Azzai disagreed. The most important verse, he said, is "Human beings are created in the image of God." Ben Azzai continued in his response to Akiva: "You say 'Love your neighbor as yourself' is the most important verse. What if you don't love yourself? How then will you treat your neighbor?" There must be a baseline of self-love, and therefore, he reasoned, the most important verse must be "Human beings are created in the image of God."

Foundational Narrative

You remember the work of creation. You are mindful of all that You have made. You unravel every mystery; all secret things are known to you. For there is no forgetfulness in Your Presence, nothing hidden from your sight. You remember every deed. You know every doer. All things past and present are known to You, Eternal God, and every person's acts are remembered.

High Holiday liturgy

Guilt

I, David, am standing next to a friend who is dying much too young of cancer. The cancer has spread, and there is no treatment left to save him. I can hold his hand, but that does not relieve the pain he is feeling. He is one tough guy, a hard-driving lawyer who can tear witnesses apart. He turns to me and asks if God is punishing him for his sin, that he had slept with his assistant a few years earlier and he is filled with shame. I know how much he loves his family, devoted to his wife and his kids, how he would protect them with his whole being. I know the good he has done, the generosity of his spirit in caring for others. But now, as he lay in bed, his physical suffering was overwhelmed by his sense of guilt and shame that he has been living with for years.

There are so many reasons to feel shame, and not just for our own lives. Years ago, we were asked to keynote at a conference on secrets, family secrets of addiction, of violence, of abandonment, of depression—the untold stories, hidden from sight and yet so present and painful. The conference was meant for directors of preschools in our region to help navigate what we know are the dysfunctions that afflict so many. But when invited, one director after another said, "Those are not problems in our school, in our community." But, of course, we all knew that wasn't the case.

Abba Eddie, our father and father-in-law, had heard our conversations about addiction and its costs. He commented that this seemed irrelevant to the lives of most people. But then, when reminded that as a child of the Depression, his parents out of work, he would hide under the bed hugging the wall, hoping that he was far enough in to avoid his father's drunken anger if he should swing a belt at him. That memory was sobering as he began to consider the ways that he and his siblings and mother had hidden the story, and the lifelong costs of the silence for all of them.

We try to protect ourselves by not sharing our own secrets that haunt us: our failures, our struggles with alcoholism or addiction, our depressive moments, our rejections, our need for help, for food, for assistance. We understand that the secrets we harbor become sources of shame. It is those things we cannot say to ourselves that have power over us. Once we can say them, own them, and if, we want, share them, they no longer control us. We are free. For real, know the truth, and it will set you free. Our attempts to protect ourselves and hide from our secrets create a shell of hardness around us, with shame and an erosion of self-worth only growing inside us more.

We all have secrets. The child who finds out that her father had another family who perished in the Shoah/Holocaust. The gay son who finds out that his father had been a cross-dresser. The mother whose bulimia and unspoken eating disorders are playing out among her children. If in God's sight nothing is hidden, then when we turn to God in prayer we can be honest and open our hearts. And as God forgives, we can forgive ourselves.

Perhaps the deepest secret so many of us harbor is that deep down we feel we are not worthy, we are not beautiful, we are not good or loved. In the early years of teaching, I, David, had a nightmare, except it was during the day, as I imagined myself standing in front of a class of adult learners. I would finish my presentation, and then someone would ask me a question for which I had no answer. He would then stand, point his finger at me, and say, "I knew you were a fraud." And my pants would fall down to my ankles, forcing me to waddle off the stage, head bent in shame. It was not, of course, an outer voice speaking to me. It was my own voice, one of fear that if only I were truly known, not just as a teacher, but as a human being, then everyone would know that I am a charlatan.

We are worthy. We are created with a spark of the Divine. Our baseline is that we are created in the Divine Image. We are worthy of change, and we *can* change and become more loving and better people. In this work of change, of *teshuva*, we often come face-to-face with shame that we harbor inside. Shame is an obstacle to change. We have done wrong, yes, and we bear responsibility for what we have done. We have lied and cheated; we are not liars and cheaters. We have done bad things; we are not bad people. We have failed; we are not failures. Shame keeps us from seeing ourselves as worthy and able to change.

When we forgive ourselves, we release ourselves to begin the process of change. We hold our own soul within us with compassion. And in having compassion for ourselves, we will be more gentle and more compassionate with those around us. We need to unearth the secrets we have buried within ourselves—at least to God. God can handle it. And so will we. And when we see that our children or grandchildren are struggling with issues with which we have struggled, what once we may have seen as a source of shame and brokenness may instead, in sharing, be a gift of wholeness and repair.

Rabbi Nachman of Bratislav suffered with depression his entire life. He was no stranger to self-doubt. He offered this profound and exquisite instruction about the process of *teshuva*, beginning with self-forgiveness:

> You have to judge every person generously. Even if you have reason to think that person is completely wicked, it's your job to look hard and find even the smallest bit of goodness. When you find that bit of goodness and look at the person *that* way, you really may raise her up to goodness. Treating people this way allows them to be restored.
>
> So now, my clever friend, now go do it for yourself as well. I know what happens when you start examining yourself. "No

goodness at all" you find. Watch out, my friend, for Old Man Gloom who wants to push you down. This is one of his best tricks. You, too, must have done some good for someone sometime. Now go look for it. But then you find it and you find fault with it. "Even the good things I did," you say, "were all for the wrong reasons." Then keep digging, I tell you, keep digging, because somewhere in it there was indeed a little bit of good. That's all you need to find: just the smallest dot of goodness. That should be enough to give you life, to bring you back to joy. By seeking out that little bit even in yourself and judging yourself that way, showing yourself that *that* is who you are, you can change your whole life and bring yourself to *teshuva*. It's that first little dot of goodness that's the hardest one to find. The next ones will come a little easier, each one following another. You can rescue your own good spirit from all that darkness and depression.[3]

Sometimes when we don't believe it, asserting that we are worthy, that we are deserving of love, is an act of faith. Our Torah's first and most fundamental teaching about human beings is that we are each created *b'tzelem Elohim*, in the Divine Image, each of us unique and infinitely precious. To change, we must first assert that we are worthy of change.

In the world around us, we are assaulted daily by messages that denigrate human dignity, that aim to humiliate us with assaults on our identity—our age, our ethnicity, our color, or our occupation. We each need to be valued and cherished, not in spite of who we are, but because of who we are. Not in spite of our limitations, our lack of ability or vulnerabilities, but because we are human. Knowing and accepting ourselves as fully human, we can see those whom we encounter as human and worthy of our compassion and gentleness.

What about those who have hurt us? Are they, too, worthy of our compassion? Our gentleness? How do we deal with the hurts against us?

The traditional path of *teshuva* moves us from honest self-reflection, owning and taking responsibility for the wrongs we have done, to genuine apology, and finally, we hope, to changing our behavior. What about those who have hurt us? What is the role of forgiveness of others in this path of *teshuva*—a path of transformation?

What can we learn from Phyllis Rodriguez and people like her, people who have suffered from inconceivable violence and injustice and still have found the resources within to forgive? Most of us have not had to deal with the murder of a loved one—but we have had to deal with betrayals and dishonesty, disappointment or hurt, abandonment, abuse or neglect. Is forgiveness a possibility we even want to consider?

Perhaps your muscles are tightening right now as you are wondering: Would forgiving this person mean admitting that they were right and I was wrong? Would it mean that I would have to keep swallowing the intense anger I often feel toward them? That I would have to pretend that they didn't hurt me? So, first, let's talk about what forgiveness is not.

Forgiveness is *not* condoning inappropriate behavior—your own or anyone else's. Abuse, violence, aggression, betrayal, and dishonesty are just some of the behaviors that may be completely unacceptable. It is not about letting people off the hook for what they have done. You may feel that firm and decisive action—divorce, litigation, or leaving a relationship—is called for or even required to prevent the behavior from happening again. Forgiveness does not mean you approve of or support the behavior that has caused you pain, nor does it preclude taking action to change a situation or protect yourself. You might forgive your parent for being too critical; that doesn't mean you start confiding in them all over again.

Forgiveness is *not* assuming an air of judgment or of pity. If I forgive my brother for failing to show up yet again and participate with the family by telling him, "I forgive you. Forget about it; I didn't think you could get it together anyway," then I have covered my deep disappointment, even hostility, in a charade of forgiveness.

Before we address the question, so what *is* forgiveness? let's talk about why we forgive. The first answer is the most selfish: holding on to anger and resentment is like giving someone you hate rent-free space in your brain. Some of us hold on to angers against a person who has long since died. Who is suffering? Who is being punished? The first reason to let go of anger is that it consumes us, it eats up our life, it constricts our growth, and our spirit shrivels up and dies.

Anger at first is useful. It is a flag, calling our attention to emotions that run deeper. Underneath our anger can be feelings of powerlessness, of hurt or abandonment, fear or frustration. Is our anger a calling out for attention, for acknowledgment, for caring? Peeling away the layers, we see that anger was the flag at the surface, not the essence of our feeling.

Forgiveness is a decision to see beyond the limitations of another person. In the same way that Judaism asks me not to see myself as I am, but as I might be, so is the case in seeing another. In 1922, Walter Rathenau, Germany's foreign minister and a Jew, was killed by three right-wing, anti-Semitic assassins. The police tracked down all three; two committed suicide and the third, Ernst Techow, was captured. A short time later, Rathenau's mother wrote this letter to the mother of the murderer:

> In grief unspeakable, I give you my hand—you of all women most pitiable. Say to your son that, in the name and spirit of him he has murdered, I forgive, even as God may forgive, if before an earthly judge your son makes a full and frank confession of his guilt... and before a heavenly judge repents. Had he known my son, the noblest man earth bore, he would have rather turned the weapon on himself. May these words give peace to your soul.[4]

What strikes us most in this letter is her willingness to see the murderer beyond the particular circumstances of his life. "Had he known my son, the noblest man earth bore, he would have rather turned the weapon on himself." Forgiveness begins with the willingness to see—to envision a world beyond the limitations of the moment.

What Mrs. Rathenau may never have known in her lifetime (she acted independent of any possible outcome) is that she

> had a belated but profound effect on Techow. Released from prison for good behavior after serving only five years, he soon found himself in a Germany ruled by the Nazis.... However, Techow came to truly repent his anti-Semitism and his horrible act. In 1940, after France surrendered to Germany, he went to Marseilles and helped more than seven hundred Jews escape to Spain with Moroccan permits.... As he remarked to a nephew of Rathenau's, whom he happened to meet: "Just as Frau Rathenau conquered herself when she wrote that letter of pardon, I have tried to master myself. I only wished I would get the opportunity to right the wrong I've done."[5]

As long as we hold on to the angers against those who have hurt us, they don't need to deal with themselves; we are doing all the emotional work of dealing with their wrongdoing. Releasing them not only releases us from the anger that eats us up, it also frees them to start taking responsibility for their own lives. Mrs. Rathenau freed her son's murderer to deal with himself, and in the process affected the freedom of hundreds of others.

Why else forgive? Because we, too, are not perfect. We are not only not perfect; we are also capable of terrible things. We are capable of betrayal, dishonesty, indifference, cowardice, and aggression. Aleksandr Solzhenitsyn wrote, "If only there were evil people somewhere insidiously committing evil deeds, and it were necessary only to separate them from the rest of us and destroy them. But the line dividing good and evil cuts through the heart of every human being and who is willing to destroy a piece of his own heart?" It is because we are so reluctant to face the potential for evil within that it is easier to hate someone else, to be angry with someone else.

Renata Stih and Frieder Schnock, world-renowned artists, stood at the entrance to the Bavarian Quarter in Berlin, winter 2013, welcoming our group of New York Jewish travelers to their permanent installation in this former Jewish neighborhood. Strategically placed throughout the neighborhood are street signs based on Nuremberg Laws, gradually constricting daily life for Jews in the 1930s to an impossible existence: "Jews may not sit on this bench, or buy bread at this bakery before 4 p.m." We were already primed for self-righteous anger. Renata spoke to us: "I just returned from your country," she said. "I had an installation in Atlanta, Georgia. I was standing in a major square—and there was a huge tree in that square. People were hanged from that tree," she said, and continued: "I didn't see any signs there. You all have a lot of work to do."

Our immigrant families harbored deep resentment against the German people for the atrocities of the Shoah. How, they asked, could decent people have seen what was going on and not done something? But now we also must ask ourselves, if someone were to knock on our door in the middle of the night, and letting them in would certainly put our own family at risk of death, would we let them in? We, too, are far from perfect. Germany, in a way singular in our global community, has taken responsibility for the reign of terror it inflicted on the world, even though few of its perpetrators are still alive. For those of us whose families were victimized or killed during the Holocaust, forgiving Germany means that we recognize our own limitations to act with courage in the face of terror.

Many decades ago when I, David, was in my late teens, I traveled in Germany, the country from which my mother had fled as a teenager and at whose hands much of our family perished. I was then a college student, and an encounter took place in the student dorms in Heidelberg, the summer after the 1967 War in the Middle East. Why was I going to Israel? the German students wanted to know. What did it mean to travel into conflict? I shared with them the stories of my family, the stories of survival and escape, the stories of capture and death. The German students began to share their stories of the Holocaust and World War II, one by one—until one of them broke down, sobbing. His father, he said, was a member of the SS and had been killed on the Russian front. "He died before he had a chance to repent," his son, the student, said, "and now his sins are mine to carry."

For how long will I—will we—refuse to forgive? Jewish tradition teaches that if someone comes to us once, twice, and three times—and we still refuse to forgive, they need not ask anymore. Why do we refuse to forgive?

And we don't mean just the Germans. We often believe deep down that it is righteous to hold on to our anger. We deserve to be angry; we've been hurt time and again.

Forgiveness is not condoning terrible behavior; terrible things have been done to us. Forgiveness can't happen before we acknowledge our deep hurt. There is no shortcut past the pain and the grief. But in refusing to let go of our anger, in refusing to forgive, we chain ourselves to our suffering. We remain perpetual victims. We remain, in our minds, neglected children, betrayed lovers, a persecuted people. It would help us as individual people to be more open to the possibilities of forgiveness.

We traveled to South Africa the summer of 2006 to learn from Helen Lieberman, an extraordinary woman who was and is the guiding spirit of Ikamva Labantu, a grassroots organization caring for literally hundreds of thousands, an organization born during the horrors of apartheid. We expected to learn from her and, even more, we expected to learn from those most oppressed. When we stepped off the boat onto Robben Island, the prison where Nelson Mandela was incarcerated eighteen of the twenty-seven years he was in prison, the first thing we saw was a large sign with these words, written by a fellow prisoner:

> While we will not forget the brutality of apartheid, we will not want Robben Island to be a monument of our hardship and suffering. We would want it to be a triumph of the human spirit against the forces of evil, a triumph of wisdom and largeness of spirit against

small minds and pettiness, a triumph of courage and determination over human frailty and weakness.

—Ahmed Kathrada

Former wardens, as an act of repentance, together with former prisoners, serve as guides at Robben Island, acknowledging that, while certainly very different, all were victims of the apartheid regime. Archbishop Desmond Tutu, the chair of South Africa's Truth and Reconciliation Commission, said,

> When I talk about forgiveness, I mean the belief that you can come out the other side a better person. A better person than the one being consumed by anger and hatred. Remaining in that state locks you in a state of victimhood, making you almost dependent on the perpetrator. If you can find it in yourself to forgive, you are no longer chained to the perpetrator.[6]

From the bitter conflict in another part of the world, between Irish Protestants and Catholics, comes an echo of this same understanding: "I'm beginning to realize," said the daughter of a man killed in an IRA bombing, "that no matter which side of the conflict you're on, had we all lived each other's lives, we could all have done what the other did."[7]

If only that essential human wisdom would permeate the tragic and intractable conflict in Israel and Palestine. That is the hope of the Parents Circle Families Forum, seven hundred Israeli and Palestinian families, bereaved from the ongoing conflict, whose courageous work—meeting person to person, family to family—is now in its thirtieth year. Ten years ago, Robi Damelin and Bassam Aramim—a Jewish Israeli woman and a Palestinian Muslim man—walked to the front of the Congregation Kol Ami sanctuary on the holiest day of the year, Yom Kippur. Each had lost a child to the ongoing conflict—a bereavement of unrelenting sadness. They came on Shira's invitation to speak to the community about pain, about forgiveness, about hope, about peace. Thousands of people were in attendance. Most had never met a Palestinian, not to mention a Palestinian who knew more Hebrew than they did! Most had never seen a Palestinian and Israeli who were friends, who shared pain, who trusted and supported each other. People were already weeping just to see the two of them walk to the pulpit together. Forgiveness and reconciliation are so much more powerful than anger. The Parents Circle Joint Israeli-Palestinian Memorial Day, the annual ceremony of remembrance and hope, born of vulnerability and shared pain, draws a quarter of a million viewers worldwide. The only path toward peace is through forgiveness and reconciliation. Every other path leads to an unending cycle of violence, anger, and revenge.

And closer to home, in June 2015, twelve people were shot during Bible study at Mother Emanuel AME Church in Charleston, South Carolina. The parishioners, all of whom were Black, had already invited the white man who had walked in to join them. They were welcoming, generous, and unassuming. Twelve were shot; three survived. Two days later, the survivors of the tragedy spoke of forgiveness. The spiritual power of that forgiveness reverberated with unbelievable force. Nothing, until that moment, had convinced the state of South Carolina to remove the Confederate flag from the state capitol. That forgiveness was so powerful that no force of hate or bigotry could survive in its presence. Polly Sheppard, one of the survivors, shared her thoughts about forgiveness in a live TV interview three years later:

If Felicia could forgive—and she lost her son—then why is it so hard for me, that I can't forgive? From that day on, I had a release, because forgiveness is like—you think you're letting someone else off the hook, but actually you are letting yourself off the hook, because if you keep it, there's no healing.

What can we learn from these remarkable people?
What would we be like if we were more forgiving?

Forgiveness is about empathy and compassion. And often, the person most in need of our compassion is ourselves. "It is we who inflict injury upon the self."[8] In our tendency to denigrate ourselves, we are hardly alone. We are all so critical and judgmental—not just of others, but also of ourselves. We are also in need of compassion—compassion for ourselves. We forgive others to release ourselves from the chains of anger and victimhood; we forgive ourselves to release ourselves from the chains of self-denigration and shame.

We are in need of healing. Forgiveness is not an act we do once, and there, it's done and over. Forgiveness is a process, perhaps lifelong, a cultivation of deep self-knowledge, of profound responsibility for who we are and what we have done, of recognition that we and everyone shelter a spark of the Divine within, and of the compassion that will release us from the sins of the past and liberate us to become the people we may yet be.

Rabbi Nachman of Bratislav taught that people reach in one of three directions: out to each other, up to God, and within to ourselves. The miracle of life, he said, is that in truly reaching in any one direction, we touch all three. When we reach deep moments of empathy and compassion, when we find we are able to forgive others and forgive ourselves, we also find that the life-giving Presence of God moves through us.

Last Conversations

Jacob was on his deathbed. He called his son Joseph to his side. Holding Joseph and his sons close, Jacob lifted his hands and placed one on each of his two grandchildren and blessed them:

> "The God in whose ways my fathers Abraham and Isaac walked, the God who has been my shepherd from my birth to this day, the Angel who has saved me from harm, bless these two lads. And may my name be recalled in them."
>
> Genesis 48:15–16

Then he instructed them, saying,

> "I am about to be gathered to my kin. Bury me with my fathers [and mothers] in the cave which is in the field of Ephron, in the land of Canaan...." When Jacob finished his instructions to his sons, he drew his feet into his bed, and breathing his last, he was gathered to his people.
>
> Genesis 49:28–33

And Joseph? He buried his father, as his father had wished, in the land of Canaan, Israel. He returned to Egypt,

> where he lived to see children of the third generation.... At length, Joseph said to his brothers, "I am about to die. God will surely take notice of you and bring you up from this land to the land God

promised to Abraham, to Isaac and to Jacob… and when God has taken notice of you, you shall carry up my bones from here."

Genesis 50:22–25

The Torah records the stories of the lives of our founding families—the conflicts, the deceptions, the loves and anguish, the births and deaths. And in these stories that close the book of Genesis, the Torah tells us how the great patriarchs prepared for their dying. The Torah records the clear instructions they gave to their children. They each invoked the story of the generations that came before them, and each gave of their own blessings while entrusting to their children the unfolding of the future. Past, present, and future—all in a powerful, singular, and explosive moment of life. All infused with God's Presence, a sense of purpose and destiny.

There are many who, at the threshold of death, cannot bless those whom they leave behind. For some, death takes us suddenly; for others, the end of life robs us of our capacity to know, or to articulate, our hopes and our deepest feelings. And still for others, we are afraid to talk about our dying, and we miss the chance to say our blessing— to bestow upon those who survive us our deepest blessing.

And so our religious traditions invite and encourage us: don't miss the chance. You will not live forever, and there are precious opportunities right now. We understand that it might spook us to talk about death. We fear that it might jinx us, or that it will compromise the quality and joy of our life right now. We don't want to talk about saying good-bye.

But good-bye is built into the fabric of life. It doesn't matter when it happens. Bringing our first, or last, child to nursery school. Taking leave of our parents—or old friends—wondering if we'll ever see them again. Making the decision to move—closing the door on one part of our life and opening a door to the next. Walking a child down the aisle of a wedding. One more child off to college. We love with all our hearts, knowing all along we will have to say good-bye.

And so in these joyous moments—when our children spread their wings, a fiftieth anniversary, a new birth—when we are so happy, we are also crying. Why do we cry? Because we also know it is so fragile, so fleeting—it is only a moment. Their life and ours. Here but for a moment.

In the years when our own children were already grown up but before they were married with children of their own, we found ways to be together, mother and son, as adults. With Noam, it was a week in Berlin, during the year that he was living and studying there. We shared the space of his studio—an intense week of immersion into his life in that city. The last night, we were sitting on the floor of his apartment, playing cards, when Noam suddenly spread a bunch of cards in his palm and said, "I've chosen a card," he said. "Now tell me what card it is." I looked at him like, are you kidding me?

"Concentrate," he said. "I'm focusing on it, so concentrate."

I did. I ventured, "The two of spades." He turned the card around. The two of spades.

"Now you do it," he said.

"Can't we just quit while we're ahead?" I said.

"No, you do it."

So I spread out my hand and I chose the card—and focused on it.

"Easy," said Noam, "the queen of hearts."

We were in perfect sync. Timeless. Without age or generation. A moment out of time. And then I remembered that I was going to say good-bye. And in an instant, I was again the mother. Saying good-bye is what we do. We love with all our hearts, knowing all along we will have to say good-bye.

It is so fragile, so fleeting—it is only a moment. Their life and ours. Here but for a moment. And so we hold on. We hold on to the times they were young—or the times we were young. Or we are filled with fear of the future—what if… ? What if he won't always love me? What if she leaves me? What if something terrible happens? We know the nightmares. We either wish for a past that is no more, or we are frozen in fear because of what might someday be. And we miss out on life.

So here's the craziness. Let go of it—and you will have it. Like the kids' song, hold on to love, and you won't have any. Hold on to spiritual power—claim it for yourself—and you have none. Share it, give it away—it will be part of you.

It's not only love we hold on to. We hold on to anger. We hold on inside to those who have hurt us, refusing to forgive them, thinking we have power over them as long as we refuse to grant them pardon. But we have no power until we let it go. Until we release them, and relinquish all control, we will not be free to live. As long as we are afraid of losing, or of saying good-bye, of letting go of hurt or anger, we will not be able to fully embrace now. As long as we expect to live forever, as long as we expect that we will not suffer, that people we love will not get sick or die, we will always be unhappy and disappointed. If we hold on to the hope that nothing bad or sad will ever happen to us, our lives will be without joy. As long as we live in fear of dying, we will not be able to live. And we are going to die. "I'm not afraid of dying," Woody Allen said. "I just don't want to be there when it happens."

What would happen if we were there, really there, as much as we could be? Jacob was on his deathbed. Holding Joseph and his sons close, he blessed them.

A few years ago, the synagogue received a call from someone outside the Kol Ami community who wanted to know if I could help with the impending funeral of a friend. I didn't feel at that time that I could. Would I be willing to talk with her? Yes, I said. The phone call came in; we were connected. I turned away from my computer screen, closed my eyes, and listened. It was easier for me to listen than usual. I had no preconceptions, no baggage. I didn't know what she looked like; we had no history. I had no agenda. I just listened. She was expecting to die within days. Why the call? She was furious at her family—her family of origin. They had not spoken for decades. Should she speak to them before she died? she wanted to know. Should she take that risk?

There must have been some crime, some act of violence, some irreparable damage. I imagined terrible things. But then I really couldn't imagine. I said to her, "I have no judgment about your anger. I do not know what your family did to you. I am sorry for the pain you bear. I have no judgment," I repeated, "on whether you should or shouldn't reach out. Only if you do, who knows what impact your reaching out might have long after you die?"

There was only one question I knew in that moment to ask: "Do you want to die with this anger?" I asked her. She answered in a flash. "No," she said. After that, she needed no help, no advice.

I wouldn't have known what happened next, but in the way the world turns, her funeral ended up being at my synagogue. I learned that she had been gay, and had loved and lived with a woman for decades. Her family had rejected her. (It's hard to imagine how our hearts have changed and opened, for many of us only in the last few decades.) She grew older, never speaking with her brothers or parents, never meeting her nieces and nephews.

She chose to reach out to her family. I learned that she died with her nieces and nephews all around her in her bed—and her brothers vowed to carry on her legacy of openness and inclusion.

We think that the end of our lives represents only loss and diminishment. There is unbelievable power at the end of our life, concentrated power, that will last forever in the lives of those we leave behind.

"I'll miss you so much," I said to Rosanne, what turned out to be the last night of her life. "You will find me in your heart," she said to me. And because she said that to me, it is so much easier for me to find her in my heart. The blessings we give at the end of our lives last forever.

"When I was a second-year student at HUC-JIR," writes Shira Stern,

> I began volunteering at Memorial Sloan Kettering Cancer Center, focusing on pediatrics, although I covered other floors when the need arose, especially when other chaplains were away. One particularly cold winter Friday, I was preparing to go home to make Shabbat, when I noticed a mislaid request for candles and wine to be delivered to a patient's family. Coat on, sunset imminent,

I wrestled with myself: "It's late already; someone should have taken care of this; will they even still be there if they are Shabbat observant?"

Gathering wine, challah rolls and electric lights, I made my way to the room, where a middle-aged woman was sitting just outside the door. In broken English, she thanked me for coming in, and when I responded in French, she began her story. They were recent immigrants from Syria and had traveled from the other side of the world to make a better life for their two teenage sons, buying into a business with the husband's brother. Two months later, her husband was diagnosed with stage-four liver cancer, and he was given little hope of recovery. She cried when she said this, cried harder when she wondered how to raise fatherless children, and wailed because she felt so alone. All the unsaid words a couple might share over a lifetime needed to be articulated now, but her husband had been semi-comatose for days; it was too late.

Her two sons, sitting in chairs on either side of the bed, were studiously ignoring our conversation. I suggested we usher in Shabbat together, so I set up the lights on the bedside table, poured the wine, covered the rolls with a clean towel, and then drew the privacy curtain around us. Rivka asked that I lead, while she held on to her husband's feet. I sang softly so as not to disturb the quiet in the room. As I lifted the Dixie cup to chant Kiddush, the patient lifted his hands and placed one on each boy's head, reciting both the traditional blessing for sons (the blessing of Jacob for his grandchildren), as well as *Yivarechicha*—may God bless you and watch over you. His wife stood stunned, unable to move. When I began to sing, the man sang with me, quickly, and without missing a beat.

When it was over, every one of us was in tears, and I left them to savor the moment.

By the time I had reached the lobby, the man had died."[9]

Jacob was on his deathbed. He lifted his hands and placed one on each grandson's head. Someday, he said, all of Israel will bless their children as I bless you now.

There is incredible power as we prepare to die. Undeniable, raw power at the end of life. And that power is right now—right here. Some of us may be dealing with an imminent terminal diagnosis—but all of us are vulnerable. Life is precious for each one of us. Thinking about our dying could scare us to death, or it could free us up to live. And difficult conversations with those we love are sometimes the most liberating.

Ritual / Spiritual Practice

Palliative care professionals share this wisdom—there are five things we need to say to someone before they die: Thank you. I love you. I forgive you. Please forgive me. Good-bye.

Religious traditions invite us to do the same:

I forgive you. Please forgive me. We find the people with whom we share our lives; we ask forgiveness, we forgive.

I love you. Find your power to bless. You have the power to bless others, to see the spark in them and to gently blow on the spark and give it life. You can bless your children, your friends, your partners. And the words of our traditions help. This blessing was and is still known as the Priestly Benediction, but it belongs to all of us. Jewish traditions bequeath this blessing as a Sabbath ritual with which we bless our children and one another.

> *Yivarechicha Adonai v'yishmirecha.*
> May God bless you and watch over you.
> *Ya'er Adonai panav eilecha viychuneka.*
> May the light of God's Grace shine on you.
> *Yisa Adonai panav eilecha v'yasem l'cha shalom.*
> May God be with you and bless you with peace.

I forgive you.

Please forgive me.

I love you—the power you have to bless.

Thank you.

"I don't remember much about my Bar Mitzvah," writes Rabbi Ed Feinstein.

> I don't remember more than a few words of my Torah portion, or what the rabbi said to me, or what I wrote in my Bar Mitzvah speech. But I do remember quite vividly the Bar Mitzvah that took place in our shul the week after mine. That boy, my classmate and friend, had lost his father to cancer just weeks before. His family decided to go ahead with his Bar Mitzvah. After reading his Torah portion, he stood before us and spoke about his gratitude. He shared gratitude for the time he spent with his dad between the bouts of chemotherapy, for the support and love of his mother and sister, for the kindness of the community. I remember that speech clearly, and I remember how he stood composed and resolute before the congregation as all of us wept. We wept for

the sadness of his loss. And just as much, we wept out of wonder for the depth and wisdom he reflected. The human condition is terribly fragile. And the only remedy for this fragility is our gratitude. Gratitude is the only thing stronger than our fear and our sadness.[10]

We don't have to wait for the last minute to say thank you. We can begin every day, every morning, with thank you. "I thank You for reawakening my soul within me." We do not own our life; we don't deserve it, we're not entitled to it. It is all gift. All of it. *Modah Ani.* I thank you.

And good-bye? How do we say good-bye?

Jewish tradition offers a prayer that we can say before we die, or that someone can say on our behalf.

> My God and God of all who have gone before me, Author of life and death, I turn to You in trust. Although I pray for life and health, I know that I am mortal. If my life must soon come to an end, let me die, I pray, at peace. If only my hands were clean and my heart pure. I confess that I have committed sins and left much undone, yet I know also the good that I did or tried to do. May my acts of goodness give meaning to my life, and may my errors be forgiven. Protector of the bereaved and the helpless, watch over my loved ones. Into Your hand I commit my spirit; redeem it, O God of compassion and faithfulness.

Just as we have a way to say thank you every morning, we have a way to say good-bye every night. And why say good-bye at night? Yes, we don't know if it will be our last. Yes, to come clean, to be at peace. But maybe most of all, to say, I will not fear. Life is too great, too incredible, too great a gift. And if we are consumed with fear of dying, we will miss it. I love you and bless you. I thank you. I forgive you. Please forgive me. Good-bye. We say good-bye so we can live.

Spiritual Practice / Ritual

Prayer can emerge at any moment, in any place. The space between moments, these border states known as liminal moments, can be the grand moments of life's transitions: a wedding, giving birth, facing death or serious illness. The regular and daily transitions of life are also liminal moments—waking up and going to sleep. These quotidian moments, moments of transition and openness, are prime moments for prayer in every religious tradition. Nighttime and preparing for sleep are universally understood as times of vulnerability: sometimes of concern and worry, sometimes of reflection, sometimes of calm and peace, often a time of openness. This short prayer from Jewish tradition steps into that liminal unknown with words of reassurance and comfort.

A nighttime prayer:

B'yado afkid ruchi, b'eit ishan v'a-ira
V'im ruchi g'vi-ati, Adonai li v'lo ira.
Into Your hand, I place my soul—when I sleep and when I wake.

In body and in spirit, in life and its passing,
You are with me; I will not fear.

4

קדושה

Kedusha / The Sacred

A LIFE OF WONDER

Nourishing a Heart of Gratitude

Foundational Narrative

It is good to give thanks to the Eternal and sing to Your name.

Psalm 92:1

Spiritual Expansion

It is gratefulness that makes the heart great.

Abraham Joshua Heschel

As a rabbi, I have been privileged to be part of so many birth ceremonies. Parents and grandparents of babies have stood before family and friends, naming their children with the ancient rituals and with beautiful poems and songs. In joy, they express their deepest hopes for them. What I've heard so often was, "The only thing I want for my child is to be happy."

Each time, I was struck by that phrase. Live your life without sadness? We try our best. We try so hard to insulate children from pain and protect them from tragedy. We keep them away from sick relatives in the hospital, and fret over their attending the funeral of their grandmother, lest they meet up too directly with grief and separation. But, "Fearful of getting hurt," notes Harold Schulweis,

> our pain threshold is increasingly lowered. The smallest irritation, a traffic jam, long lines at the theater, are intolerable. We grow anxious before every challenge, we fear any disappointment, any defeat. From infancy we are raised to avoid pain, to instantly stop the headache.
>
> And we have found the cure. Open up the sacred chest. Open up the holy ark—the medicine cabinet of our homes—and behold a pharmacopoeia of potions and pills promising salvation. More than twenty billion dollars a year spent on sleeping pills, stomach settlers, headache tablets and pain killers.... Marx claimed that religion is the opiate of the people. The inverse is more accurate. Opiate is the religion of the people.[1]

We do want to be happy. But happiness does not come by avoiding pain.

As parents, we certainly had fantasies about the perfect childhood. It did not take long to realize how complicated and, in some fundamental way, silly it is to imagine a life without struggle, without pain.

Little Zachary just would not speak, not a word since he was born. Parents, therapists, doctors—no one could coax him to speak. Of course, the parents panicked. Then, three-year-old Zachary was sitting at the table and tasted his bowl of oatmeal. "It's burning my tongue," he screamed. His parents were elated, breathing a sigh of relief as they gave him a glass of cold water. "You spoke, Zachy. Why now?" The three-year-old gave the simplest answer: "Because everything was perfect until now."

We think about this often, how to engage the world, knowing there will be pain. In our zeal to create the perfect security blanket, a force field to protect those we love from hurt and sadness, we all are robbed of the chance to be more human.

Living also hurts. Giving birth also hurts. And giving birth to ourselves also hurts. To be fully alive is to allow a place to feel pain—to struggle, to wrestle, to fail, to reach for the stars.

The Buddhist tradition provides a metaphor that, while recognizing pain and suffering in human existence, also knows that life is to be lived with equanimity, that death is entwined with us daily:

> Life at birth is like being a wave that rises on the ocean. When we die, the wave sinks back into the ocean. But the consolation is that water itself doesn't disappear, and with new energy, the wave emerges from the depths of the sea again.

It is an extraordinary irony that the discovery of joy begins by letting go of the hope that we will live forever—by letting go of the expectation that we will never suffer, never experience loss or grief or pain.

God's Been Good to Me

Our family went to visit St. Paul's Community Baptist Church in East New York. We first learned about this church in Samuel Freedman's award-winning book *Upon This Rock: The Miracles of a Black Church.* East New York is not exactly the Garden of Eden. Sam Freedman, a longtime journalist with the *New York Times,* had decided during his work with the church that he would like to give them a daily gift subscription to the *Times,* only to discover that although the *New York Times* delivered around the globe, it did not deliver to that section of New York City.

People line up around the block for services, 1,500 at each of three services, and we, and our young children, lined up with them. The service doesn't begin with anyone asking the congregation to stand or sit—you come into a sanctuary filled with music. And when everybody is finally on their feet, singing and clapping, then the music slows and everyone sits down. And the music had been so tremendous that morning, that as soon as everyone was seated, Reverend Johnny Ray Youngblood said, "Sounds like God's been good to somebody here!" And everybody was back on their feet again, hollering and clapping.

Sometimes you have to go someplace else to learn something about your own tradition. Later in the service, the pastor turned to his congregation and said, "Turn to someone and tell them, 'God's been good to me.'"

Simple. Personal. No fancy language. We know many of us don't usually talk that way; it sounds pretentious, the words hard to believe.

And besides, my week was not so great. But there it was: God's been good to me.

Later that week, we're sitting together for family dinner, and we're about to say grace after our meal, which we sing in a somewhat repetitive, predictable, nonconscious way. It's pretty; the singing and the harmonies are great—but it has little to do with God or gratitude. And then we look at the words.

Baruch she-achalnu mishelo uv-tuvo chayinu.
Blessed is the One through whose goodness we live.

We live through God's goodness. I live because God is good to me. But we never said it like that—God is good to me.

Perhaps at this moment, it's easy for me to say, "God's been good to me." We are healthy. Our children and grandchildren are healthy and thriving. But it won't always be like this.

Does that mean, then, that God is no longer good to me?

God's goodness has nothing to do with living forever, or living without pain. We're the ones who want to live forever and can't think of what to do on a free Sunday afternoon. So often, we don't know how to be grateful for the moment we have now. God's goodness has nothing to do with living forever. God's goodness has to do with living now.

Spiritual Practice / Ritual

The Vietnamese Buddhist monk Thich Nhat Hanh teaches about this quality of paying attention to the moment. When he introduces a mindfulness workshop with children, he first draws the children close and does an exercise with them of making watches out of paper.

They fasten the paper watches to their wrists, and then the monk asks them, "What time is it?" The answer, of course, is that the time is now.

Our sages of old wrote hundreds of blessings for moments of wonder—and they are a life-giving inheritance to all. In fact, the sages taught that if we don't have a hundred reasons a day to stop in amazement, we aren't living fully awake; we've been sleepwalking. Sometimes we can't miss it: a gigantic clap of thunder, the brilliant turn of autumn leaves, blossoming trees and rainbows. And Judaism has blessings for all of these.

But a lot of the time, in the most ordinary of moments, we miss it. We miss that we're alive. And so there are blessings for ordinary moments: eating an apple, putting on new clothes, waking up in the morning, going to the bathroom (a place of countless spontaneous prayers), blessings for learning, blessings for grief, blessings for joy. Experiencing something for the first time: Blessed are You who has kept us in life and enabled us to experience this moment. Not the huge miracles—just this moment. Being able to feel God's goodness means letting go of living forever. It starts with living in the moment, in spite of the fact that it won't last forever—because it won't last forever.

Please—think for a moment about your life. No matter what else is going on, think about a blessing in your life. Whatever it may be. Blessings of insight. The miracle of newfound strength. Of pleasure in the colors of autumn. Of love in your life that you have experienced. Of love you have given. Of friendship. Of understanding. For having brought comfort or encouragement to someone else. Of waking up this morning. Of blessing this very moment. For the baseline gift of life. Let the blessing you have chosen flow over you.

Forever

Years ago, the mother of a close friend was dying, and my mother decided that I should go visit her for Shabbat—candles (unlit), wine, bread, and guitar. I, David, went grudgingly, bringing Noam, then about five years old, to sing the blessings with me. Claudia made it clear that she was not religious, never went to synagogue, and was content enjoying all the pleasures of the world. Still, it was a beautiful moment, surrounded by family, the sun setting. She asked everyone but me to leave. Claudia spoke about her life, her sadness at dying so soon, and then, reflecting on the first Shabbat she celebrated in her life, she said, "I will remember this forever." It was a shock: what could "forever" mean to a woman on the verge of death?

Hers was a deep understanding. Forever. She was preparing to die. She was not denying her death. "I will remember this forever." Life is not forever, but a moment fully lived is, somehow, forever.

She decided that the following week she would celebrate the second Shabbat of her life in the hospital. Sixty-five friends, relatives, and hospital staff, including her oncologists, gathered together late Friday afternoon in a room prepared by her hospice team. Lights, wine, challah, song and blessing, loving and sacred spirit. She spoke of her life, the blessings, the trials, her beautiful family. I taught a melody and then sang the Hebrew words of Reb Nachman: "The world is a very narrow bridge; the essence of life is not to be overwhelmed with fear." As the Shabbat celebration was ending, her final words were voiced again: "I will remember this forever."

At the funeral, all those who had shared her final Shabbat were there, and they sang the words, that life is a very narrow bridge and the essence is not to be overwhelmed with fear. When we focus our energies on living forever, we instead let life itself slip through our fingers. But when we let go of the hope of living forever, we actually begin to live.

Blessings can bring us back into the moment, back into life. Noticing a moment. Blessing it. Making it sacred. All amazement, that we have ever been alive. No matter what else is going on in your life—no matter what. That we can think, that we listen deeply to a friend, that someone feels known or cherished in our presence, that we can be amazed at the smallest detail (did you know that bananas are divided lengthwise into perfect thirds?). We have so many reasons to bless a day.

The Cable Car

There is practically not a person who has visited San Francisco who has not ridden its fabled cable cars. But most don't get down on their hands and knees—no, not to kiss the ground, but to peer through the metal guides that run along the center of the street to the cable down below. The cable always runs, and in order for the cable car to climb and descend the steep streets of the city, it latches on to the powerful cable below the street and the cable pulls it up.

We often imagine God in that way. It is the transcendent movement through all of life. It is always moving—ever present and eternal. But it is not out there or over there or way up there. It runs through everything. Every moment is imbued with the transcendent. In the language of Judaism, every regular moment can be *kadosh*, or holy. *Kadosh* is when you grab on to the cable—tap into the transcendent.

Biting into an apple can be a nonthinking, instinctual thing to do when you're hungry and holding an apple. Or it can be a moment in which we choose to let ourselves be aware of the wonder of life, of body of color and taste. A moment. The blessing is a way we latch on to the cable, a way to connect with the transcendent and holy.

Underneath it all is the mystery and miracle of life itself. The ultimate gift. For which we say, a hundred times, forever, amen and amen.

Spiritual Practice / Ritual

Judaism offers an accordion of blessings for moments large and small. Many can be found in the appendix of this book. We include one here, a blessing for noticing or doing something for the first time in your life—a blessing for the gift of life itself.

Baruch ata Adonai eloheinu melech ha-olam, she-hecheyanu v'kiyimanu v'higiyanu lazman ha-zeh.
Blessed are You, Source of the Universe, who has given us life and sustained us and brought us to this moment.

5

מקום

Makom / The Presence

A LIFE OF OPENNESS

We Are Never Alone

Foundational Narrative

Moses said, "O, let me behold Your Presence!"
The Eternal answered, "I will make all My goodness pass before you, but you cannot see My face, for a person cannot see Me and live." The Eternal continued, "*Hinei makom iti.* There is a place for you with Me. Station yourself on the rock, and as My Presence passes by, I will put you in a cleft of the rock and shield you."

Exodus 33:18–22

In every place [*makom*] where I cause My Name to be mentioned, I will come to you and bless you.

Exodus 20:21

Foundational Narrative

Jacob left Beersheba and set out for Haran. The sun was setting; taking one of the stones of the place, he made it his headrest and lay down. He dreamed; a ladder was set on the ground, with its top reaching to heaven, and angels of God going up and down on it.... Waking from his sleep, Jacob said, "Truly, the Eternal is in this place, and I did not know it."

Genesis 28:10–12, 16

Spiritual Expansion

"God was in this place." In what place? Perhaps Jacob thought that the place was where he slept, for he then poured oil on the rock and anointed the place. There is another possibility: where was the place of Jacob's dream, the place where he encountered the Presence? It was in *him*. When he awakens from the dream, Jacob says to himself, "Truly, the Eternal was in me—and I did not know it."

We might be looking for God in the wrong places. We look in some of the "obvious" places, the ones with holy names on the outside. But, as Alice Walker in *The Color Purple* reminds us, people ought not come to church to find God; they should come to church to share God.

How might we find God?

The Kabbalists, and mystics of many traditions, offer a beautiful metaphor, a Jewish mystical story of the cosmos. Imagine that the essence of God is love—Infinite Love. In the beginning, that's all there was. But there's a problem. If what you are is love, then you need to be loving; you need to have something to love. God can't be love if there's nothing to love—and all there was was God. And so the Kabbalah teaches that God withdrew into a single point of infinite density. God—Infinite Love—contracted into this single point of infinite potential, an act they called *tzimtzum*, and then exploded into every direction, pouring Divine light into material creation.

This, of course, sounds much like the cosmological view we know as the Big Bang. In the beginning was the Big Bang. Fifteen billion years ago, a single point of infinite density, of infinite potential—containing everything that now exists—exploded spontaneously in all directions. Energy cooled. Photons (elements of light) for the first time were freed from the building blocks of matter. Matter and radiation had decoupled, and the universe turned visible. "Let there be light! *Yehi or!*" Glimmering balls of hot gas formed into stars. Combining and recombining. Carbon, oxygen, iron, copper, silver, tin, iodine, gold, mercury, and lead—cycling and recycling into new systems, forming and exploding, creating our galaxy, our solar system, and our planet. As one physicist exclaimed, "We, along with everything else, are literally made of stardust."

We have learned from physics that there is no real difference between matter and energy; everything is on the same continuum—matter is energy slowed down. The mystic would say that the same is true of Divine light and material creation. We are Divine light slowed down. Moses Cordovero, one of the mystics of Safed, wrote, "Do not say, 'This is a stone and not God.'" Divine energy permeates all creation. It is all God. Divine energy is concealed within all creation. *Ein makom panui minei*. There is nothing—no thing, no moment, no person—devoid of Divine Presence.

The mystical tradition teaches that God isn't out there. God doesn't reside in the heavens any more than God is here. There is nothing that isn't God. You are made of God. You are made of the stuff that exploded out of the Big Bang, and that same energy pulses through your body and floods your soul. There is a God-spark in everyone and everything: the rock, the moon, the sunset, the ocean, you and me.

When we talk about God, we often get stuck with this opening question: Do you believe in God? Perhaps a better question is: What do you imagine when you think about God? A preschool teacher described to me a conversation that took place as her students were painting out in the yard. She paused next to one particularly abstract work and asked the three-year-old, "What are you painting?"

"I'm painting a picture of God," he responded.

To which the teacher quickly responded, "But, honey, no one knows what God looks like!"

The preschooler put down his brush for a moment and looked up at her. "When I finish," he said, "they will."

Visions of God are personal and are to be respected, but not all visions of God are productive. We know this from our own lives as parents.

The Bathtub

When our youngest child, our daughter Liore, was two and a half, David was giving her a bath. Out of the blue, she looked up at him and said, "God likes boys better than girls." I know for sure that had it been me giving her the bath, I would have quashed that one right away. I would have said, "Oh, no, sweetheart, that is not true!" But

David was wiser. Instead, he asked her, "What makes you say that?" Liore answered, "God has a penis and boys have a penis, so God likes boys better." In our religious tradition, God is not gendered. There are no pictures of God in our home. We didn't realize—before that moment—how powerful the pronoun can be. We spoke of God as "He," convincing ourselves that "He" was neutral—neither male nor female. As interesting as that was, what we learned most from that bathtub encounter was far more important. What we learned is that because Liore imagined God as male, she imagined herself as somehow worth less in the universe. How we imagine God makes a huge difference in how we see ourselves.

The mystical traditions invite us to see ourselves as part of God. These traditions teach that the beginning of sin or wrongdoing is when we see ourselves as separate from God. When we see ourselves as part of God, we see we are not separate from anything and that everything is interconnected. Because we are all connected, everything matters; every individual act affects the whole.

Returning from a trip to Morocco, we got the crazy idea to turn our bedroom into Santa Fe—or Morocco (they share certain architectural designs, like beamed ceilings). It didn't take long to figure out that, between the cost of buying beams, the difficulty of getting them into the house, and the expense of putting them up without bringing the house down, the whole project was out of the question. But in the process of crawling around the attic space above our room to see what kinds of supports already existed, our carpenter friend called down to us, "You won't believe this—but you already have the beams." And the whole project became just taking down the ceiling and exposing the beams.

Sometimes it's been there all along—and you just have to remove the obstacles so you can see it.

A Precious Gem

There once was a man who had a precious gem. Before he died, he showed the gem to his daughter. Together they decided to bury it in the backyard to keep it safe for future generations. They marked the spot with a stone. When the daughter was about to die, she told her eldest child about the gem. She added a stone and instructed him to remember the gem and to mark the spot with a stone before he died. Father to daughter to grandson to great-granddaughter followed the custom, each generation adding its stone until an enormous pile of stones marked the spot. But no one remembered that buried underneath was a beautiful and precious gem.

So many religious services are overwhelmed with lengthy liturgy, cherished words and rituals. In a tradition as old as Judaism, each generation has added its layer of words to our prayer books—until the piles of words, ceremonies, and rituals we have built up have totally obscured the spiritual gems that are buried underneath. In fact, most of us don't know or don't believe that spiritual gems are actually anywhere to be found in these rituals and words, even when we faithfully follow them.

This story spoke to me, Shira, very directly. I loved this story of the buried gem—all those stones, these words and rituals, piled on top of buried spiritual treasure—because, as it turns out, I have long had a mistrust of words. The first moment of childhood rebellion I remember—I might have been six or seven years old—I was very upset about something and was having trouble explaining myself. My mother said to me then (she surely would not say it today), "If you can't say it, you don't know it." And a little voice inside me said clearly, "That's not true."

There is a knowing that is deeper than words.

This spiritual wisdom returned to me as an adult. My father died at the close of a June Sabbath just after my fifty-ninth birthday. I have been present in so much loss that it was shocking to me how strange and new was the terrain of the death of my own father. I had traveled back and forth to Israel for years to visit and spend time with my parents in Jerusalem—intensified in these last years by my father's life-threatening illnesses. On so many of those flights, I thought about and dreaded the time that my flight would be to my father's funeral. It was late Shabbat afternoon when we got the call. My father had been in a coma for seven weeks, the result of a terrible fall. My siblings and I had already gathered by his bedside a month earlier (that time together prepared us to be more tender and present for one another at the time of our father's funeral).

As the plane lifted off from New York at the close of Shabbat, with David seated next to me, my mind in a daze, I felt in a rush all the moments of loss and comfort I have experienced in my life. I kid you not; a totally unexpected rush of energy rose up from all the love. It was like a river suddenly shifted course and rushed toward me. It felt like *that* was the energy that lifted the plane up and off the ground and carried me, with David, to Jerusalem.

But once the plane lifted off with love, it was that daze of death that took over. Burial in the hard rock of Jerusalem's hills; the blur of people coming in and out of my parent's Jerusalem home; and back home, here, for the conclusion of shivah, the week of mourning. I was grateful to have been surrounded with love, to hear the harmony of voices in prayer, to be held and assured. But the daze of death is strong.

I sat up in bed later that night—motionless. A blank face. A hand moved down across my expressionless face. My own. "You cannot sign that way, with a blank face," I heard my sign-language teacher say. And before I had time to think—from a place deeper than words—my hand leapt up in front of my face with the sign for "mad." My face was no longer expressionless. I was mad. I was angry that my father had left a trail of longing. I was angry at the pain. I was angry at him—and angry at myself—that neither one of us had the courage to talk about painful things together. And then I started to cry.

Over the years, I have immersed myself in the study of American Sign Language. Long attracted to this beautiful, dance-like, strong language, I did not know that the study of sign would hold other lessons for me. In my childhood home, intellect ruled. You had to know it in order to say it. But not in sign. Hands moving are not enough; you have to feel it in order to say it. You simply cannot sign with a blank face.

There is a place deeper than words. It is a place where spiritual gems are buried. And they are so often covered up with words.

Prayers and liturgies sometimes connect us to the sacred. But sometimes the piles of words obscure a spiritual gem hidden underneath—and we need to clear some space.

The Jungle Monastery

Whenever we take a trip, no sooner are we home than we are putting together another trip just like it—to bring along as many people as possible to experience some of the things we've experienced. When we returned from this sabbatical journey, we could not even put together a short list of people whom we thought would be interested in going where we had been.

Dear Friends,
Thank you for your recent letter. On behalf of the abbot and the monastic community, I would like to cordially welcome you to our monastery to study Buddhist meditation…. I'm not sure how familiar you are with our tradition and form of Buddhist training, so I have enclosed a few books that you may find useful to read before your visit.

So opened the letter from Wat Pah Nanachat, a Buddhist forest monastery located in Eastern Thailand, not far from the Cambodian border. It would be part of a journey into the life of the spirit—to learn more about how other peoples understand the religious search, to learn more about ourselves, and to find out what from this an observant and dedicated Jew might bring into her and his life. David went off to the men's section of the jungle monastery.

"This is your *kuti*," the woman explained to me. My cabin, where I was to spend much of the next week, was barely the size of our mudroom back home. Four walls. Screen windows. A tiled floor. Nothing more. I thought that at least there would be a mattress!

I was directed to a storeroom where I would find a grass mat, a blanket—and what looked like a large black pillowcase open at both ends that would be my skirt.

So, first, the pretty story:

The gong goes off at 3:30 in the morning. It's easy to get dressed—you only have one outfit to wear. I wind my way—as others do, each from separate areas in this forest jungle—along the forest paths, a walk of twenty or thirty minutes to the other side of this expansive forest monastery. In the open *sala*—the gathering area—monks are already seated on the marble floor in their dark orange/brown robes, hand-dyed from the barks of trees. Behind them are the novices in their white clothing—and behind them, the students and few visitors. At the front, a large Buddha image—and orange candles glowing against the darkness. It is stunning. Quiet. Only the sounds of the forest jungle. The early morning breezes, the chanting of the monks, and an hour of silence.

The day begins in this way—in the middle of the night. With dawn, the service ends; the monks prepare to walk through the nearby village, barefoot on rocky dirt roads, to accept whatever gifts of food the villagers offer them, while the novices and visitors sweep the pathways of the forest. With the return of the monks—each from his own alms rounds—the food is prepared, and the community gathers (it is now 8:00 in the morning) to eat the one meal of the day.

Now the not-so-pretty story:

The gong goes off at 3:30 in the morning. It is easy to wake up (I'm not sleeping all that soundly in the first place). It's not easy to put on that skirt sarong and keep it on. It's about three feet wide, and there are no belts, pins, or drawstrings. I head out—with my pocket flashlight in hand—into the night of the jungle. I have a really bad sense of direction. Really bad. And there are many paths through this jungle. There was not one morning that I didn't lose my way—alone—in this dark jungle. It was terror.

I tell you this story because there was an even greater terror. Getting lost in the night of the jungle became a metaphor—a metaphor for a different kind of unending darkness. Much of the day is lived in silence. There is some chanting, but mostly meditative silence. The one meal of the day is eaten in silence. Though one does walk past others, one is discouraged from engaging in conversation. Though David (who, I later found out, was deeply immersed in an extraordinary meditation experience) and I saw each other over these days, we hardly spoke.

And to my surprise, I found the experience of hour after hour, night after night, one day followed by yet another—of silence—to be a different kind of terror. Like the night, it was endless, and I didn't know how to find a path through it.

But after a few days, I finally began to hear my own voice. I began to actually hear it—because there was no one, and nothing, to distract me from it. There was no one to blame, no one to deflect it to, no one for me to project it onto. It was finally there for me to hear. And I did not like a lot of what I heard.

We swept the pathways of the forest each morning as the monks left on their rounds. I swept my pathway out with religious fervor (realizing that the white clay of the cleared path would help me find my way out). I memorized the landscape, the curves of the pathways, the bends of the trees. And on the last morning, I got lost again. But for the first time, I did not panic. I actually laughed out loud. I couldn't believe that with all my preparations, I had actually gotten lost again. I knew this time that I would find my way out.

And, like the forest, I learned that I would find a way through the endless unknown of silence.

We were so sure that this was a trip on which we could not bring anyone else along. But we were wrong. We do want to bring you there. There *is* a place where we can go. Into the unexplored and initially strange terrain of silence. "*L'cha dumiya tehila*. To you, O God, the highest worship is silence." We live in a world overflowing with words cascading from one device after another, pounding us with high-volume commercials, a cacophony of sound.

"*L'cha dumiya tehila*. To you, O God, the highest worship is silence."

The Bible, the Tanakh, tells us a story about the prophet Elijah. Elijah was perhaps jealous of some of the great prophets who had come before him. He knew that Moses, after forty days atop Mount Sinai, had witnessed fireworks and lightning and the blast of the ram's horn and God's thundering Presence. And so Elijah, generations later, set out for the mountain of God, walking forty days and forty nights. "Then the word of the Lord came to him. God said to him, 'Why are you here, Elijah?' Elijah replied, 'I am moved by zeal for the Lord.' 'Come out,' said the Eternal, 'and stand on the mountain before Me.'"

> And lo, the Presence of the Eternal passed by. There was a great and mighty wind, splitting mountains and shattering rocks by the power of the Eternal; but the Eternal was not in the wind. After the wind—an earthquake; but the Eternal was not in the earthquake. After the earthquake—fire; but the Eternal was not in the fire. And after the fire—*kol d'mama daka*—the sound of

stillness. When Elijah heard the sound of stillness, of total silence, he wrapped his mantle about his face and went out and stood at the entrance of the cave. Only then a voice called to him: "Why are you here, Elijah?"

1 Kings 19:9–13

Religious settings have been the home of majestic music, the requiems of Mozart and Beethoven, Mahler's Resurrection Symphony, Muslim Sufi, Buddhist, and Hindu chants, the gospels of the African American church. Yet we have learned that there is also another pathway to spiritual experience.

"*L'cha dumiya tehila*. To you, O God, the highest worship is silence."

Buddhist monasteries and Catholic convents, mindfulness retreats and Hindu ashrams, Quaker services and Jewish meditation—all share an understanding that one of the pathways to a profound and deeply felt experience of Divine Presence is silence.

There is no need to travel to a jungle monastery in Thailand to find an inner voice. One need not learn sign language to understand what is felt deep inside. We can cultivate a practice of quiet, of calm, of mindful attention. There is no prayer book; there are no words. No thunder and lightning, no fireworks, no blast of the shofar. Just stillness. Clear—empty—quiet.

Spiritual Practice / Ritual

One of the beautiful names for God/Eternal is Makom. "Makom" means "place"—in this case, the One Who Is Present in Every Place. Or, in the words of the Kabbalists, "There is no place devoid of the Presence." *HaMakom*.

We sometimes need places and physical touchstones in which to remember and notice. In some religious and cultural traditions, people create a small shrine in their home, a constant reminder of the sacred.

In Jewish tradition, we place this reminder at the entrance/exit to our homes. Crossing the threshold, entering—or leaving—our homes, we are reminded of our connection to the sacred. The words of the Torah can speak to any of us: "Take these words which I command you this day and place them on your heart. Teach them to your children. Speak about them when you rise up and when you lie down. Write them upon the doorposts of your house and on your gates" (Deuteronomy 6:5-9). These biblical words are traditionally written on a scroll and rolled up inside the case (the mezuzah) which is affixed to the doorpost at the entrance of the home.

If you were to adopt and adapt this tradition, what other verses, poems, or phrases would you roll up inside the mezuzah case? Where would you place it?

Spiritual Practice / Ritual

Pablo Casals, the world-renowned cellist, marked the sacred space of his home in this way:

> For the past eighty years I have started each day in the same manner. It is not a mechanical routine but something essential to my daily life. I go to the piano, and I play two preludes and fugues of Bach. I cannot think of doing otherwise. It is a sort of benediction on the house. But that is not its only meaning for me. It is a rediscovery

of the world of which I have the joy of being a part. It fills me with awareness of the wonder of life, with a feeling of the incredible marvel of being a human being. The music is never the same for me, never. Each day it is something new, fantastic and unbelievable.[1]

If this ritual speaks to you, what music would you choose to bless the day? Would you play it? Would you listen to it? Would you sing it?

Spiritual Practice / Ritual

A Blessing for the Home

May the door of this home be wide enough to receive all who hunger for love, all who are lonely for fellowship.
May it welcome all who have cares to unburden, thanks to express, hopes to nurture.
May the door of this home be narrow enough to shut out pettiness and pride, envy and enmity.
May its threshold be no stumbling block to young or straying feet.
May it be too high to admit complacency, selfishness, and harshness.
May this home be, for all who enter, the doorway to a richer and more meaningful life.
(Adapted from Rabbi Sidney Greenberg)

6

צדקה

Tzedaka / Justice

A LIFE OF RESPONSE

Reaching beyond the Self

Foundational Narrative

God (in the story of the imminent destruction of the cities of Sodom and Gomorrah): "Shall I hide from Abraham what I am about to do, since Abraham is to become a great and populous nation and all the nations of the earth are to bless themselves through him? For I have singled him out, that he may instruct his children and their children to observe My ways by doing what is just and right."

Abraham then came forward and said,

> Will You sweep away the innocent along with the guilty? What if there should be fifty innocent people within the city; will You then wipe out the place and not forgive it for the sake of the innocent fifty who are in it? Far be it from You to do such a thing, to bring

death upon the innocent as well as the guilty, so that innocent and guilty fare alike. Far be it from You! Shall not the Judge of all the earth deal justly?

Genesis 18:17–25

Mordecai to Esther:

Do not imagine that you will escape with your life by being in the king's palace. On the contrary, if you keep silent in this crisis, relief and deliverance will come from another place, while you and your father's house will perish. And who knows, perhaps you have attained to royal position for just such a crisis.

Esther 4:13–14

You know the heart of the stranger, because you were strangers in the land of Egypt.

Exodus 23:9

Spiritual Expansion

It is not your obligation to complete the work; neither are you free to neglect it. (Pirkei Avot 2:16)

Spiritual Expansion

Autumn leaves. It turns out that green is the color that hides the natural colors of leaves. Leaves inherit their colors in much the same way that we inherit hair and eye color. The inherited colors of certain maples, for instance, are orange and yellow. The activity of chlorophyll throughout the spring and the summer produces the green color of these leaves. In the fall, as the chlorophyll dies back, the green "recedes," revealing the inherited colors of the leaves—the colors that, in a sense, were there all along. It turns out, then, that the leaves don't "turn" different colors; instead, as the frost of fall descends, they are showing their truest colors.

We love observations like these. For one thing, they turn the way we see the world upside down. Nothing has changed in the observable data; all that has changed is the way we see it. Another reason that we love this particular observation is that it provides a beautiful example of a profound religious and mystical teaching. There are so many realities hidden right beneath the surface. We only see them when, for one reason or another, the surface peels back, revealing what was there all along.

Sometimes the surface peels back and we are able to see for a startling instant that God was there all along. These may be moments of joy or birth, of extraordinary beauty, or simply seeing a friend unexpectedly walk into the room just when that person had come to mind.

What about suffering? Is God hidden within suffering as well? Where is God when terrible things happen? There is an infinity of answers to these questions; we hold no monopoly on truth. We offer a lens through which to view these questions—with a story.

Tsunami

Our daughter, Liore, went to India to volunteer with a group of women who wanted to create a community enterprise selling shoes. In the hot and humid Tamil Nadu south, she not only helped them build a website presence, she also taught women's health and how to open a bank account. We traveled to India to witness her efforts and then swept her away to a small resort on the beach of Mamallapuram for a brief respite. It was Christmas 2004, and we enjoyed the celebrations with Santa Claus waiters and snowy Christmas carols performed in sweltering Hindu India. The next morning, Liore and David went for a run on the beach. Returning for breakfast, we were sitting at the table when we heard screams and saw a wall of water churning toward us. It was what we now know as the Asian tsunami, with waves reaching thirty meters, sweeping away 250,000 lives throughout Southeast Asia. We ran, hearing exploding computers and kitchen utensils clanging, climbed the closest hill, swept forward by the waters, and witnessed one of the largest natural disasters in modern history.

"How could God let such a disaster happen?" was one set of voices we heard. Others, in hearing the story of our survival, wrote that God must love us, protecting us from the waves even as so many others died. These words were of no comfort. The tsunami was a natural disaster, the result of tectonic shifts deep under the sea, part of the evolution of our earth. This undersea earthquake struck in Indonesia. It would be hours before the tsunami hit the coast of India. Only the poorest of the poor lived at the edge of the ocean. There were no sensors in the Indian Ocean; there was no early-warning system on the coast. No one in India needed to have died.

Thirty thousand people lost their lives in Tamil Nadu; whole villages were destroyed. When Liore went back to begin rescue work, all that was left of the village where she and David had run a few days before was a gnarled concrete staircase. Everything else was gone.

Asking "Where was God?" in the aftermath of the tsunami's destruction is a deflection, a way to avoid the more urgent and pressing questions: Where were the sensors, the warning sirens, all those whose actions could have limited the tragedy? Blaming God is the language of indifference. Believing in a God who acts because we don't is using God as an excuse for our apathy and inaction.

We need a different view of God.

Let There Be Light

In a moving and tragic episode of *Little House on the Prairie*, a beautiful young woman is finally overcome with blindness, the result of disease they could not prevent a century ago. A handsome young man (this is television) wants to calm the overwhelming sense of panic she feels. He takes out a book written in Braille—in rural America, that would have been either an alphabet primer or a Bible. It was a Bible, and he opens to the first page. He places her hand upon the bumps, and then his hand on hers, as he moves across the page and reads aloud: "In the beginning there was darkness and chaos. And the spirit of God moved across the darkness and God said, 'Let there be light.'"

Twenty-five hundred years earlier, the prophet Isaiah proclaimed God's message: "I created you to be a light to the nations. To bring light where there is darkness. To liberate the oppressed and bring the captive out of confinement. I created you to lift up the fallen, to clothe the naked, to feed the hungry and redeem the oppressed" (Isaiah 42). "God" is when our hands move across the face of the darkness, when we feed the hungry and free the captive. God is hidden. Disguised. God masquerades as you and me.

World War II and the Holocaust were a watershed event for many in the Jewish community, challenging their faith in a caring and present God. "Where was God?" is a mantra of despair we hear often. If we shift our focus, however, we might ask a different question. Why, in the face of such overwhelming danger, why did anyone reach out to help? Johtje Vos, a non-Jew who hid thirty-six Jews in Holland, responded to that question:

> Two questions are always asked of us. One is, why did we help Jews during the war, and the other is, would we do it again? Now, to the last question, I have a very easy answer. I don't know.... Why did we do it then? Well, my husband and I never sat and discussed it or said, "Let's go help some Jews." It happened. It was a spontaneous reaction, actually. Such things, such responses, depend on fate, on the result of your upbringing, your character, on your general love for people, and most of all, on your love for God.[1]

She did not ask: "Where is God?" It is we, who sit by the sidelines, who ask, "Where is God?" Some images of God are more likely to obscure, rather than reveal, the loving Presence of God. A vision of God who acts in the absence of human initiative—a God who acts because we don't—is using God as an excuse for our apathy and indifference. We do not believe that God is up there and we are down here and that God acts upon us as a king upon his subjects, or who sits in judgment upon us—judge, arbiter, defense, prosecution, witness, all wrapped up in one. The danger of imagining God in this way is that we can remain little children, shaking in fear of a punishing parent, instead of growing up and taking responsibility for ourselves and our world. Why did God do this? and Why didn't God do that? rob us of moral responsibility. Imagining God as distant and separate from us, we blame God for the terrible things that happen in the world instead of taking responsibility for them.

We are the ones who know about genocide, and torture, and political corruption, and hunger or domestic violence, or the trafficking of women and children. We are the ones who know. I want to find the God of whom I am made who could work through me and through you.

The mystical traditions invite us to see ourselves as part of God. These traditions teach that the beginning of sin or wrongdoing is when we see ourselves as separate from God. When we see ourselves as part of God, there is no one or nothing to blame. The responsibility and the agency are ours. Once the surface peels back, we see that we are not separate from anything and that everything is interconnected. Because we are all connected, everything matters; every individual act affects the whole.

Jewish life, like many cultures and traditions, has a holiday of masquerade. Its heroine is Esther, herself living a hidden life. In a pivotal moment of the story, Esther has the opportunity to reveal her identity—to show her true colors—and to save her people from impending disaster. The risk, however, is great, and Esther is reluctant. Her cousin Mordecai sends this message to her: "Do not imagine that you will escape with your life by being in the king's palace. On the contrary, if you keep silent in the face of this crisis, relief and deliverance will come from another place, while you and your father's house will perish. And who knows, perhaps you have attained to royal position for just such a crisis" (adapted from Esther 4:13–15).

God is glaringly absent from the telling of this tale. The Hebrew language has a word for God's hiddenness. It is *hester*. In a perfect linguistic twist, the Hebrew name of the biblical heroine, Esther, is linked to God's hiddenness. In a time of God's hiddenness, we need to step forward and act. In a time of *hester*, we must be *Esther*.

Hidden. We wonder who it is who is hiding.

I remember, early in our marriage, when times were difficult, how David would lie in bed next to me, but facing the other direction—his back what felt like an insurmountable wall between us. It took a long time for me to see that I was the one putting up the wall, that I had projected the emotional distance inside me onto him. Perhaps the same is true with God's hiddenness. Perhaps God is hidden from us when *we* put up obstacles—in the same way that we can block the sun by putting up our hands in front of our faces. Perhaps God is hidden when we turn away and do not see.

The Elephant and the Tsunami

We fled inland from the waters of the tsunami along with tens of thousands who were as shaken as we were. Before we returned to the United States, and before Liore returned to relief work, we sought out the calm of Periyar National Park, a magnificent oasis of mountainous jungle in the heart of India. Walking down a hill of tall grasses and huge gray boulders, our tribal guides suddenly stopped in their tracks. "Shhh," they signaled. "There's an elephant." We looked with excitement, but were confused. What elephant? The guides pointed. Apparently there was an elephant not ten meters away from us, among the tall grasses and huge gray boulders, well camouflaged. We do not remember exactly how long it took us to see it—close to ten minutes. Do you know what it's like to be standing ten meters from an elephant and not be able to see it?

There are many ways not to see. A friend of our family who directed UNICEF operations was visiting us for Shabbat lunch. In talking about his work, he said that in the developing countries, fifteen thousand children under five die every day for lack of food, water, and medicine—without any change in the foreseeable future. Fifteen thousand children a day; more than a hundred thousand children every week. A tsunami of loss—twice every month. Right in front of us, and we don't see it. "In the face of the enormity of that tragedy," someone asked, "why do anything?" "The choice," he said, "isn't ending poverty. The choice is turning away and doing nothing, or doing a little."

It's the same with us. The choice is to turn away and do nothing, or do a little. "God" is when we see that we are all connected; "God" is when we understand that God has no hands but ours. "God" is when we are appalled that one in six children in America will go to bed hungry tonight—and we do something, however small, about it. "God" is when we work to ensure that a person working full time at minimum wage can actually make it in America. "God" is the outrage when our government continues to cut public services for the poor and provides tax cuts for the rich. "God" is the irrational courage to love in the face of inevitable loss, in the face of separation or disappointment, in the face of death. "God" is the knowledge that life matters, and that we, like Esther, are alive at this time, in this place, for a reason.

It is a simple truth—one we often choose to ignore—that everything is connected to everything else. The story is told of a wealthy and miserly man whose beautiful estate was surrounded by poor villagers. The lives and fates of the villagers were of no interest to the wealthy man, and he refused to reach out with any help. One day, the village sage invited the wealthy man for a ride in his rowboat. When they got to the middle of the lake, the sage took out a hand drill and began drilling into the boat. "What are you doing?" the wealthy man cried in alarm.

"I'm drilling a hole," answered the sage.

"You can't do that! If you drill a hole, we're going to drown."

"Not to worry. I'm only drilling in my side of the boat," answered the sage.

We share a planet. Trade winds and ocean currents, viruses and epidemics sweep over our entire planet. Poverty and lack of opportunity in one part of the globe will create waves of population movement toward areas of greater opportunity. We share one planet.

That is the first reason to reach out beyond ourselves: we are all connected.

The second reason is that we don't do well alone. We are neither happy nor effective working alone in the world. Hillel the Sage taught, "If I am not for myself, who will be for me? And if I am only for myself, what am I? And if not now, then when?" Adrienne Rich adds a fourth line: "And if not with others, then how?" Yes, we are each connected to the whole; yes, we each have an obligation, in our own way, to repair the world, but the work of *tikkun olam*—the repair of the world—is work done together with others.

Heaven and Hell

The sages of old told a story about a young student who wanted to know what heaven and hell were like. An angel acceded to her request and brought her first to hell. The first thing she noticed was the food: banquet tables were laden with every possible delicacy and steaming platters of food—and delectable aromas wafted through the halls. But then she noticed the people. They were glum and bitter and miserable. And then she understood why: large wooden spoons were strapped onto everyone's arms, past the elbow, so that they couldn't bend their arms to put any food into their mouths.

When the student arrived at the entrance to heaven, she was taken aback. The scene was identical: the same banquet tables, the same delicacies and steaming platters—and the same large wooden spoons strapped onto everyone's arms. But nothing glum here. There was singing and talking and laughter—because people figured out they could feed each other.

Trying to do it alone is hell.

The studies are unequivocal: we will be happier if we deal with our challenges together. We *do* have problems—and on the whole, we keep them to ourselves. What keeps you up at night? Are you worried about your health? Are you worried about paying for good health care, or providing health care for your employees? A member of my congregation told me that her young adult son living in upstate New York was in a car accident, and though the car required major repairs, he was alright. "But," she said, "he wouldn't have told me if he wasn't. He doesn't have health-care coverage." Are you worried if your children are being bullied at school, or on the internet? Are you worried about being intimidated at work or about the security of your job? Do you worry that your adult children who have moved back into the community cannot afford to live there? Do you worry if you will leave this world better than you found it? You're not the only one. You also can't work on this by yourself. Working alone, you have little power to effect any change.

All the scientific and sociological studies come to the same conclusion: people are happier and healthier doing things together, coming together to work on problems and face challenges, and doing for others. If you do something to help someone else, you are most likely to experience a strengthening of immune-system activity, a lowering of stress, a reduction in the perception of pain and in attitudes—such as chronic hostility—that negatively affect health and damage the body. In separate research, reported in *Johns Hopkins Magazine*, "a 10-year study of the physical health and social activities of 2,700 men in Tecumseh, Michigan, found that those who did regular volunteer work had death rates two and one-half times lower than those who didn't." When our concerns are only on ourselves and our immediate family, our world shrinks—and so does our spirit. You will breathe bigger—you will expand your universe and your circle of concern—and you may discover your reason for being on this globe.

Where is God? Perhaps God is the force of life that runs through our lives—day in and day out—in the inexplicable force that gives a person the simple, heroic courage to open the door, to hide a child, to shelter a family, to move against our self-interest, against our own survival instincts—and to reach out to help. When we take off the mask, when we peel back the surface of fear or indifference, when we regain our sense of agency and our courage, we find out that God has been there all along.

7

שבת

Shabbat

A LIFE OF JOY

Heaven on Earth

Foundational Narrative

> Those who keep Shabbat and name its joy will rejoice in Your spirit. The people who set this day aside, making it holy, will be filled and gladdened with Your goodness. This day is sanctified and blessed by Your love, the most precious of days, a remembering of Your creation.
>
> Shabbat morning prayer book

Spiritual Expansion

Six days a week we live under the tyranny of things of space; on the Sabbath we try to become attuned to the holiness in time. Six days a week we wrestle with the world, wringing profit from the earth; on the Sabbath we especially care for the seed of eternity planted in the soul. The world has our hands, but the soul belongs to Someone Else.

Abraham Joshua Heschel

Lessons from Andree

We are visiting our "Swiss Grandmama" Andree who is celebrating her one-hundredth birthday. She does not travel anymore, so seeing her entails a flight to Geneva and a stay in her apartment overlooking the lake. Andree has lived alone for twenty-five years since the death of her husband. She is beautiful. In her home hangs her portrait, painted by Matisse. When the United Nations celebrated the Year of the Aging, her face was one of those on the poster. We sit on the balcony and she serves us lunch—fine china, chipped from decades of treasured use, linen napkins, no bottles or containers from the refrigerator, simple fare served with elegance. It sets such a warm tone, we linger at the table, telling stories and talking about the world. We thank her for all the special touches that made the meal so lovely, but she demurs—this is the way she sets her table even when she is alone. Andree believes that being classy is not a function of wealth or fancy restaurants. And she is right.

We return home and commit ourselves to set our table with nice dishes (OK, our youngest by now is five or so), butter served on a small dish, drinks in a pitcher, the food brought out on platters. Maybe it is only spaghetti with homemade tomato sauce, but it still can look lovely. And we take a set of inherited candlesticks and eat our dinner to candlelight and conversation. This is not Shabbat; this is Tuesday night. But these small additions transform our table from a quick stop in between school, work, play, and homework to a different ambience, a more intentional place.

Yosemite

We were coming through the tunnel that opens into Yosemite Valley. Noam, then three years old, was seated up front in his grandparents' motor home for the dramatic entry. We emerged from the tunnel, and the valley opened up before us: Half Dome to the right and Yosemite Falls to the left. The moment left Noam breathless, literally. When he caught his breath, all he could do was burst out singing: "I've got that Shabbat feeling right in this place!"

Family Therapy

A family in our community sought the help of a family counselor, an encounter they shared with us. As is the case for so many of us, pressured schedules, high expectations from work and school, myriad commitments—these determined the rhythm of life for members of the family. The family therapist listened and heard the frustrations, the impatience, the increasing dissatisfaction with life at home. "You might try setting aside some time," he said.

> Choose any time—maybe a dinner. Any evening will work, as long as you all agree. Turn off your tech devices. Make it special in some way: maybe lower the lights, use candlelight, set the table with

intention. Give everyone a moment to talk about their week—and everyone else really listen. Or just begin with a nice dessert a bit later, when the house is calmer and preparing for bed. Light the candles, invite everyone in, and think of conversation topics in which everyone can have a voice, no matter how young. And if it works, feel free to add a blessing to yourself about how wonderful it is that family members can actually enjoy each other and learn from each other about your experiences of the world you inhabit and your places in it. It's a modest beginning—but if you stick to it, week in, week out, you may find that you have shifted something important in your home.

This family therapist was onto something, actually a re-creation of ancient wisdom. We each need a Sabbath. Every human, every couple, every family, every group of close friends—everyone needs a Sabbath. As Heschel reminded us, our daily lives are consumed with production: we produce goods, we optimize and multitask. We are asked to prove ourselves every day, wherever our work life takes place; however meaningful and important our work is, we are delivering a product. The biblical story of creation, in its beautiful metaphors and symbols, imagines that when God completes the work of creation, when the "delivery" of six days of extraordinary creation is finished, God ceases from creation—and enjoys! God is able to see how beautiful and good the world is—and God blesses the day and calls it "holy."

The world is still beautiful and good and blessed—but we don't see it when our days are covered over with our unending to-do lists. One of Judaism's greatest gifts to the world is the Sabbath. It was unprecedented and remains so unique that the word "Sabbath/Shabbat," though phonetically adapted to each language, has never been translated. The pressures we feel in our lives—the expectations, the worries, the disappointments, the fears—they are all real. And so are amazement and joy. They are also real. Shabbat makes space for joy. What makes Shabbat work is setting aside regular, recurring, dependable time. It may be easier "making Shabbat" when others in your community are also doing it—whether it is Friday night or Sunday morning. Or you might choose to "make Shabbat" at another time that works consistently and dependably for you. Shabbat—however we make that time—clears away some of the obstacles and makes room for joy.

Love. Panic. Joy

I, Shira, felt completed as a mother when my adult children chose loving partners. Their marriages expanded the circle of loving of our family in ways I never could have imagined. I almost experienced it physically, like a pregnancy, like a literal expansion of loving. "Wait till you have grandchildren," people told me. "You get all the pleasure, none of the pain. All you have to do is love."

We waited for years, or so it seemed. "By the time I was your age," I told my kids, "I already had two children." (Like that helped.) "If you wait much longer," we told them, "you'll have to diaper us *and* your babies at the same time." I was done with thinking up one more esoteric question to discuss at an all-adult Passover Seder table; it was time to "bang, bang, bang with your hammer low" and jump like frogs all over Pharaoh.

And so I was completely blindsided when the birth of my first grandchild—a golden cherub—triggered a depression. How was that possible? Remember the circle, that ever-expanding circle of love? Science offered me an insightful analogy: with the expansion of the circle of light comes an increase in the perimeter of darkness. The greater the circle of light—the greater the circle of love—the more people I have to worry about, the more can go wrong, the more is at stake, the more vulnerable I am to the risks of loving.

Perhaps you think I was crazy. I certainly thought I was. Then I remembered that I had experienced that panic once before, when I was first a parent, afraid deep down that I would not live to raise my children, that I would die before they knew me (soon after replaced with the fear that once they got to know me, no therapist would be able to fix all the neuroses I had unwittingly already passed on).

Life is scary. Loving brings the all-too-real risks of disappointment or loss. But somewhere underneath it all is the mystery and miracle of life itself. This is an assertion of faith, that underneath it all is joy. Though we can't always tap into it, joy flows underneath. The amazement that we have ever been alive, that we can love and be loved.

Shabbat makes space for joy. We clear away other obligations. We turn off phones and devices that turn our attention away from the moment. We make space for joy.

Shabbat is where it all can come together.

Shabbat is the celebration of covenantal love. Week in, week out, ready or not, here it is. Shabbat means celebrating with friends, best around the table at home, but if entertaining is too much, you can order in or meet at a restaurant. If you are partnered or part of a big family, Shabbat means politely saying no to the invitations and obligations that come in. Shabbat means that a week won't go by without telling the people we love the most that life wouldn't be what it is without them. If there are children or grandchildren at the table, Shabbat means holding them, each child, blessing them and kissing them. Shabbat means regular, dependable time with those we love, those who are important in our lives. Cultivating faithfulness, cultivating commitment. Creating the space for love. There are so many ways to celebrate Shabbat.

Life—this life, with these people—is worth celebrating. Worth coming home from a hard week, setting the table with a tablecloth, candles, and wine. Worth going around the table and asking everyone to say something that happened in their week—because they are worthy, worth listening to.

Shabbat works. Shabbat works to create more time. When we are born, we are given the gift of time—of days and years. We make time for work, for errands, for chores. So often we hear ourselves saying, "I don't have time." "I don't have time to take a break, I don't have time for myself, time to read, time to enjoy." And, of course, it is easy to say, "I don't have time to create a Shabbat for myself, my family, friends, those I love." Yet, just as a gifted space planner can take a thousand square feet of open space, and by adding dividers, structures, and furniture, she can create more space than there was before, so Judaism does the same with time. Judaism is a brilliant architect of time, and Shabbat is its major work of art.

Shabbat works to create more time, by adding dividers and structures—by setting it off from the rest of the week. Shabbat works—on one condition: you have to stick to it. Like any great relationship, it doesn't work without commitment. Shabbat is the celebration of Judaism's most essential values, an extraordinary and accessible pairing of spiritual wisdom with behavior and ritual. It is true: those who observe a Shabbat—however you imagine and create it—will be blessed with joy. You can do it. You can carve regular time in your life, and by setting it apart, you will make it sacred. Everyone you include can be blessed; every person celebrated in their uniqueness, their spark of the Divine (*tzelem Elohim*) shared with others.

Spiritual Practice / Ritual

Everyone you have gathered together—whether in your home or at a restaurant or a park—can be invited to put their arms around each other and to bless one another. These words once belonged to the Israelite priesthood; they are now the inheritance of all of us:

> *Yivarechicha Adonai v'yishmirecha*
> May God bless you and watch over you
> *Ya-er Adonai panav eilecha viy'chuneka*
> May the light of God's grace shine on you
> *Yisa Adonai panav eilecha v'yasem l'cha shalom.*
> May God be with you and bless you with peace.

We learned about a powerful and succinct prescription for a Shabbat when our son Yaron was involved with Reboot, a start-up committed to experimenting with Jewish ideas. Reboot launched its Sabbath Manifesto, with ten core principles completely open to each person's unique expression:

- Avoid technology

- Connect with loved ones
- Nurture your health
- Get outside
- Avoid commerce
- Light candles
- Drink wine
- Eat bread
- Find silence
- Give back

SHABBAT / HEAVEN ON EARTH

Seize the day—carpe diem. "Live the moment!" is a mantra of our times. It would be wonderful to bring a consciousness of the present moment to everything we do, to every moment we live. But it is nearly impossible. The tasks and labors of our lives are important and demanding. Judaism offers a brilliant balance. Six days: Work! Do! Fix! Carpool! Take exams! Shop! Run errands! Change the world!

And when the sun sets on Friday, step back. Breathe, slow down, enjoy, bless the moment, restore, connect, love.

Whatever you do, the more faithfully you do it, the more it will give back.

We Are All Travelers

What do butterflies and the World Cup of 2014 have in common?

Butterflies: Each spring, monarch butterflies complete an annual migration from central Mexico to southern Canada. It takes four generations to complete the journey. The fourth generation is born in the northernmost end of the migration, in Canada or the northern United States. This one will be a super monarch, living eight times longer than any of the others. In the late summer and early fall, this one must begin the journey back home, a journey of up to three thousand miles. Home is one of a few mountaintops hidden in the central highlands of Mexico. It will make the whole journey from Canada to Mexico—to the forests in the highlands of central Mexico—to a place it has never seen before. This massive movement of butterflies has been called one of the most stupendous phenomena of the natural world. So many butterflies—hundreds of thousands—will end up clustered on the branches of the sacred fir trees that the branches are weighed heavy to the ground.

The World Cup of 2014: A paralyzed teenager wearing a mind-controlled exoskeleton kicked the ceremonial first ball at the World Cup in Brazil in June 2014. Wireless electrodes attached to the head collect brain waves, then signal the suit to move. Thoughts are translated into electrical signals.

Contractions

When we were pregnant with our third child, David's parents were traveling throughout India. March 9—weeks off from the due date we had given his parents before they left. Halfway across the globe, David's mother was touring some ancient Indian ruins. She turned to her guide and said, "Get me to a telephone. My children are having a baby." The nearest telephone was several miles away in a post office. After the guide explained the circumstances, the long line of people waiting to place a call cleared so that my mother-in-law could use the phone. Yaron had been born five minutes before; David had called home from the hospital to a waiting family who was now already piled into the station wagon to see the new baby; David's sister was locking the front door when the phone rang. She picked up the phone and heard her mother's voice—and screamed, knowing why she had called. Her mother heard the scream, and she screamed, and everyone in the post office in India burst into applause. My mother-in-law said later that she had felt the contractions.

Something connects labor contractions on one side of the globe to a parallel sensation on the other side; something makes it possible for a monarch butterfly to navigate thousands of miles to a mountaintop home it has never seen; a paralyzed teen can think "right foot move back," and those thoughts can be translated into movement; something is felt at the same moment halfway around the world. Our world—this world—is animated by so much that we do not see.

You already know that. You know that dogs hear sounds we cannot hear; bees see colors outside our visible spectrum; elephants know when a tsunami is about to happen. Our emotional energy affects our bodies; we have gut feelings; people can die of a broken heart. Yet we still think that what we see is all there is. "I'll believe it when I see it," we say.

And what do we see? We look at one another—or at ourselves in the mirror. If you change the style of clothes you wear, are you still you? If you change the length or color of your hair, are you still you?

Of course. If you break your arm or your leg, are you still you? "You" is not dependent on the color of your eyes, or skin, or hair. There is a "you" that is real, a "you" we summon in this spiritual journey.

The mystics of Jewish tradition have something to say about that "you" within. They open their teaching with this text from the Torah's story of creation of man and woman. "The man called his wife Eve, *Chava*, for she would be the mother of all the living. And God Eternal made clothing for Adam and Eve; the Eternal made them out of skin." It's a story of tenderness, God fashioning clothing for these creatures. But what was the clothing made of—skin? What kind of skin? The Hebrew word for skin, or leather, is "*or*," with the letter "ayin." The mystics read the story symbolically and deeply. The story, they suggest, is that God added skin—actual human skin—to human creatures. And what could we have possibly been before God added skin to cover our bodies? The mystics say that before that we were creatures of another *or*—we were creatures of light.

We know today that light is a form of energy. We know that light, energy, and matter are all made of the same stuff—different forms of the energy that makes up our universe. When we look at one another, we see the clothing, the hair, the skin. But there is more; we are also creatures of energy.

Tank-Top Undershirt

It was Yom Kippur afternoon—almost fifty years ago. We were graduate students in Berkeley, California, and had accepted a last-minute High Holiday job in a small synagogue in Studio City that was unexpectedly without rabbi or cantor. Services recessed in the afternoon for everyone to take a break before resuming with *Yizkor* and *Neilah*, as we do. We were exhausted. We had been used to being on the receiving end of what Yom Kippur has to offer; we had only been giving, and we were in serious need of replenishment.

We decided to go on a short walk in the neighborhood. Those who know me well know that I, Shira, have a horrible sense of direction. Twice in my life, however, being in a new or foreign place, I have known exactly where to go. This was one of those times. We came to a corner, and I said to David, "We must go left, down this street." He looked at me sort of strangely, but OK, let's go down this street. It was the San Fernando Valley—more ordinary than ordinary. Small houses, all looking the same, one after the other. Small plots of grass, evenly squared off. Concrete driveways separating the plots. We're halfway down the block when all of a sudden we hear someone screaming at us. We spin around, and there's a man standing in front of his house, yelling at us. He was overweight, unshaven, wearing a tank-top undershirt, and yelling at us. I'm thinking, "Did we step on his lawn by mistake? Should we start running?" But it seemed that running would be a mistake—so we walked toward him. He walked up to David and barked, "Do you know the blessing for *tefillin*?" David was so shocked he couldn't speak. (Unusual.) It was me, standing safely off to the side, who could speak—and recite the blessing. "Come in," he said, "and show it to me."

We walked into his small house. It was dark, all the curtains drawn. "My father just died," he said. "He died in New York. During World War II, he wrote affidavits for hundreds of people he didn't know. There were thousands of people at his funeral. This is what he left me." And he took out a tallit bag, a set of *tefillin* (prayer straps to wrap on one's arm), and a High Holiday siddur—a *machzor*. He handed me the *machzor* and said, "Show me the prayer for *tefillin*." "It won't be in this prayer book," I said. I did not explain that *tefillin* are not worn on Yom Kippur. "Then help me put them on," he said. And we did.

"We are conducting services around the corner," we told him. "You are welcome to come with us." But no. He wasn't interested. We left him there, in his darkened room, standing in his undershirt, wrapped in his father's tallit and *tefillin*, on this most holy of days. "All journeys," wrote Martin Buber, "are destinations of which the traveler is unaware."

We are all travelers; we are fellow travelers in this universe. Souls meant to bump into each other in this lifetime find their way. We each bring our struggles and our learning and our love, our own unique souls. We are fellow travelers on this journey of life, learning and sharing wisdom from our inherited traditions. There is so much more in this world than meets the eye. Those things that are most important to us, the things that make life worth living, are not quantifiable. A life of wonder, a life of connection, of love, of feeling that we are alive for a reason, of courage—these can't be measured or seen, but we don't live well without them.

Jewish wisdom and Jewish learning are endless—but the Torah teaches, don't let that stand in your way.

> This teaching that I give you this day is not too overwhelming for you, nor is it beyond reach. It is not in the heavens, that you should say, "Who among us can go up to the heavens and get it for us and impart it to us, that we may observe it?" Neither is it beyond the sea, that you should say, "Who among us can cross to the other side of the sea and get it for us and impart it to us that we may observe

it?" No! It is very close to you, in your mouth and in your heart, and you can do it.

Deuteronomy 30:11–14

No, it is not far away; it is so close. Jewish tradition has given us a road map, a guide through the universe. It has given us a way to walk the path. It comes to remind us that the mystery and the magnificence aren't only out there—they are here. Judaism comes to remind us that we can tap into it anytime we choose. Rituals are the ways we tap into it. Rituals are only pathways. But they work—if they are regular and dependable.

The Piano

Back in California, David used to begin each Shabbat by sitting at the piano and playing. It was always the same melody. Forty years ago, we made the decision to move as a family to New York for me to attend rabbinical school. It was a decision that left us two weeks to pack up our entire household—four children born in this home; countless arguments, joys, struggles, and triumphs in this home; but no time now for feelings and reminiscences.

It was Friday, and the Hertz truck was filled. Only one thing was left in the house, the one thing that needed professional movers—the piano. Friday afternoon. David sat at the piano and played that same melody. The same melody, at the same time, Friday afternoon. It was as if a walnut shell cracked open, perfectly in the middle, as did our hearts—and all the memories of all those Fridays, all those Shabbat evenings, just tumbled out. Rituals can be vessels that tap into the power of life.

The life-giving waters of Jewish wisdom flow beneath our feet, right where we live. We need a way to draw up these waters—a way to hold them—in order to irrigate and nourish our lives. Rituals are the vessels we use to draw up and channel these life-giving waters. The rituals—the practice, the doing—of living are the vessels that draw water from the well. They help shape a life of purpose and belonging, of love and reconciliation, of courage and agency, faithfulness and joy.

"It is very close to you. It is in your mouth and in your heart, and you can do it."

We inherited these rituals. The stories, however—it's the stories that have taught us that the mystery of life is right here.

We remember standing on the porch of Shira's parents' home in Jerusalem on a Saturday evening with our children—braided candle, spices, and wine for Havdalah. As we curved our fingers toward the light of the Havdalah candle, one of our kids (they all deny it) said that there is a little bit of light and a lot of shadow—and that what faces us is the shadow.

The shadow is mystery. So much of life remains unknown—magnificence and mystery. But we are also beings of light—pulsing with the love and energy out of which the universe was born. It is all God; the dark and the light, the night and the day. It is all glory—for to You belong the day and to You, the night.

CODA

A full draft of this book is off to the publisher. I am at the edge of the Arctic Circle for four nights, in search of the northern lights. It is the height of the eleven-year solar cycle, and Churchill, Canada, has the lowest amount of cloud cover, on average, anywhere across the aurora oval. So my chances are pretty good, I think. First night: fogged in, clouded over. Second night: clear, green lights in swirling patterns for hours. I am so overwhelmed, I only know I was there because of the pictures. Third night: clouded over. Last night: clouded over.

I tell myself: we control nothing but the energy we bring to a moment. I am grateful for wonder. I am grateful for the spirit of adventure and for health.

And then two hours into waiting on the last night, the skies above partially clear. White light streaks over the sky, snaking ribbons of white. One moment there's nothing, only darkness. And suddenly, electricity comes to life. Curtains of white and green, raining light. Then suddenly disappearing.

I lie down in the snow, face to the sky, solar wind sweeping the lights over me. Wash over me, I pray. Blessed are You, Creator of light.

Unexpected.

Undeserved.

A gift.

Fleeting. Now you see it, now you don't.

A moment of presence.

The holiness is everywhere. Only sometimes it lights up and you can see it.

Holy. Holy. Holy.

It is all gift.

Shira, March 2025

APPENDIX
EXPLORING JEWISH
RITUAL LIFE

Traditions for the 21st century

Judaism offers countless rituals and blessings. These are but a few. But they are foundational. Judaism's uniqueness indeed lies in its pairing of spiritual wisdom with behavior, with a way to walk the path of a Jewish life. Here is an opportunity for Jews and all those seeking ritual in their lives to connect a vibrant Jewish practice to a foundation of wisdom.

Vibrant. Creative. Spontaneous. Intellectually honest. Spiritually open. Ethically driven. What Judaism offers is precious. The essential Torah, the sacred story that the Jewish people brought to the world, changed human history: that human beings were created in the Divine Image, *b'tzelem Elohim*, that God moves through liberation, and that each of us is here to bring our own unique blessing to the world. Jews inherited the name Yisrael, God wrestlers, called to take on any authority, even God, in the fight for justice. We dare to believe that we are not locked in a perpetual cycle. Judaism stakes a claim that the world can get better.

You have a part in that story. The voices that have sustained the Jewish people are not the voices of extremism, or zealotry, or exclusion or intolerance. Our voices that call for equality, for compassion, for peace and justice are needed now more than ever. We wed these values to the rituals we offer here.

צלם אלהים

Tzelem Elohim /
A Spark of the Divine
A LIFE ON PURPOSE
You are alive for a reason

Spiritual Practice / Ritual

Find your own breath. Try for a moment to think of nothing else, just the breath that flows in and flows out of you. The breath that brings life to each cell of your body. Find your own rhythm. Miracles are as far away as breathing in and breathing out. The breath that you take in has been breathed into by everything around this globe that lives. Rich and poor. Humble and mighty. And those who have lived before us breathed into the air that we continue to take in. The Source of Life is as far away as breathing in and breathing out.

A Daily Morning Meditation—Choose Life

אֱלֹהַי נְשָׁמָה שֶׁנָּתַתָּ בִּי טְהוֹרָה הִיא. אַתָּה בְרָאתָהּ אַתָּה יְצַרְתָּהּ אַתָּה נְפַחְתָּהּ בִּי וְאַתָּה מְשַׁמְּרָהּ בְּקִרְבִּי וְאַתָּה עָתִיד לִטְּלָהּ מִמֶּנִּי וּלְהַחֲזִירָהּ בִּי לֶעָתִיד לָבֹא, כָּל זְמַן שֶׁהַנְּשָׁמָה בְקִרְבִּי מוֹדֶה אֲנִי לְפָנֶיךָ יְיָ
אֱלֹהַי וֵאלֹהֵי אֲבוֹתַי וְאִמּוֹתַי רִבּוֹן כָּל הַמַּעֲשִׂים אֲדוֹן כָּל הַנְּשָׁמוֹת
בָּרוּךְ אַתָּה יְיָ אֲשֶׁר בְּיָדוֹ נֶפֶשׁ כָּל חַי וְרוּחַ כָּל בְּשַׂר אִישׁ

Elohai neshama she-natata bi t'hora hiy

My God, the soul that you have given me is a pure one. You have created it, formed it and breathed it into me, and within me you sustain it. Some day this soul will become part of you. As long as there is breath within me, I will give thanks to You, Author of all creation, Source of all life. Blessed are You, who restores to me this day the chance to choose life.

ברית

Brit / Covenant
A LIFE OF CONNECTION
Learning to Love

Rabbi Hiyya fell ill. Rabbi Yohanan went to visit him. Rabbi Yohanan wisely asked, 'Do you want to be sick? Is your suffering important to you?' When Rabbi Hiyya answered, "No," Rabbi Yohanan placed his hands on him and healed him.

Then this same Rabbi Yohanan fell ill. Rabbi Hanina went to visit him and asked, "Is your suffering important to you?" Rabbi Yohanan said, "No," and Rabbi Hanina placed his hands on him and healed him.

If Rabbi Yohanan could heal Rabbi Hiyya, why then, when he got sick, could he not heal himself? A prisoner cannot release himself from confinement.

Talmud Berachot 5b

Spiritual Practice / Ritual

Brit—being in covenantal, faithful love—is to commit to something larger than myself, something beyond how I feel at this or that moment

Daily, Judaism reminds us to love—with all our heart, at home and on the road, when we lie down and when we rise up.

The *Sh'ma*—the declaration of the Oneness to whom we belong—is followed by these verses, and can be recited together with the opening line.

The nighttime *Sh'ma* can be recited alone—a reminder that even as adults we are held in the embrace of life and a loving Presence; or it can be a moment of closeness between parents and a child. For all her years of growing up, our youngest liked to be tickled as we sang her the *Sh'ma*, and when she was in bed and ready, she would call out, "Ima and Abba, will you tickle me Sh'ma?" The evening—every evening—closes with form and purpose. Life isn't chaotic; it is formed. It isn't accidental; it is on purpose. Life isn't empty—and neither are we.

שְׁמַע יִשְׂרָאֵל יְהוָֹה אֱלֹהֵינוּ יְהוָֹה אֶחָד

וְאָהַבְתָּ אֵת יְהוָֹה אֱלֹהֶיךָ בְּכָל־לְבָבְךָ וּבְכָל־נַפְשְׁךָ וּבְכָל־מְאֹדֶךָ: וְהָיוּ הַדְּבָרִים הָאֵלֶּה אֲשֶׁר אָנֹכִי מְצַוְּךָ הַיּוֹם עַל־לְבָבֶךָ: וְשִׁנַּנְתָּם לְבָנֶיךָ וְדִבַּרְתָּ בָּם בְּשִׁבְתְּךָ בְּבֵיתֶךָ וּבְלֶכְתְּךָ בַדֶּרֶךְ וּבְשָׁכְבְּךָ וּבְקוּמֶךָ: וּקְשַׁרְתָּם לְאוֹת עַל־יָדֶךָ וְהָיוּ לְטֹטָפֹת בֵּין עֵינֶיךָ: וּכְתַבְתָּם עַל־מְזֻזוֹת בֵּיתֶךָ וּבִשְׁעָרֶיךָ

Sh'ma Yisrael Adonai eloheinu Adonai echad

V'ahavta et Adonai Elohecha, b'chol l'vavcha, uv'chol naf'sh'cha, uv'chol m'odecha. V'hayu hadvarim ha-eileh, asher anochi m'tzav'cha hayom, al l'vavecha. V'shinantam l'vanecha, v'dibarta bam, b'shivt'cha b'veitecha uvlecht'cha vadarech, uv'schochb'cha uv'kumecha. Ukshartam l'ot al yadecha, v'hayu l'totafot bein einecha. Uchtavtam al mezuzot beitecha uvisharecha.

Hear O Israel the Eternal is One

You shall love the Eternal, your God, with all your heart, with all your soul, and with all your might. And these words, which I command you this day, shall be upon your heart. You shall teach them diligently to your children, and shall speak of them when you sit in your home, when you walk by the way, when you lie down, and when you rise up. You shall bind them for a sign upon your hand and they shall be for symbols between your eyes. You shall write them upon the doorposts of your house and upon your gates.

Deuteronomy 6:4-9

תשובה
Teshuva / Healing and Return
A LIFE OF INNER GROWTH
The Courage to Become You

לוחות ושברי לוחות מנחים בארון

Luchot v'shivrei luchot munachim ba-aron

"The whole tablets and the shattered ones rest in the ark."

Talmud Bava Batra 14b

There is a place within us for the broken pieces of our lives. Our broken dreams, our failures and disappointments, our struggles and our wounds, these too are holy. These, too, are places in which we feel life deeply and from which we bless the life in others.

Spiritual Practice / Ritual

An Introduction to the Nighttime Sh'ma

בְּיָדוֹ אַפְקִיד רוּחִי בְּעֵת אִישַׁן וְאָעִירָה
וְעִם רוּחִי גְוִיָּתִי יְיָ לִי וְלֹא אִירָא

B'yado afkid ruchi, b'eit ishan v'a-ira

V'im ruchi g'vi-ati, Adonai li v'lo ira

Into Your hand, I place my soul—when I sleep and when I wake. In body and in spirit, in life and its passing, You are with me; I will not fear.

A Prayer for Healing

Times of serious illness are also liminal moments that call out for prayer. This prayer for healing is not a petition. It reinforces a theology that God is present within us—and when people reach out to heal, God is present between us. Whatever the outcome of illness, the spiritual longing expressed in this prayer remains true and valid: Our prayer and the caring of others connect us to the heart of life. This prayer of the heart can be recited alone for oneself—or shared when visiting someone who is ill.

> In my illness, I turn to You, for I am Your creation.
> Your strength and courage are in my spirit
> And Your powers of healing are within my body.
> In my illness I have learned what is great and what is small.
> I know how dependent I am upon You.
> My own pain and anxiety have been my teachers.
> May I never forget this precious knowledge
> when I am well again.
> Bless the agents of Your healing, the physicians and the nurses,
> my community of friends and family
> with wisdom and patience.
> Their presence and dedication connect me to life itself and
> to You.
> Blessed are You, the faithful and merciful Healer. Amen

For you O Eternal, are seen face to face.

קדושה

Kedusha / The Gift of Divine Presence
A LIFE OF WONDER
Nourishing a Heart of Gratitude

טוב להודות ליהוה ולזמר לשמך עליון

"It is good to give thanks to the Eternal and sing to Your name."

Psalm 92:1

Blessings can bring us back into the moment, back into life. Noticing a moment. Blessing it. Making it sacred. Rabbi Yehuda Leib Alter of Ger, author of the book *S'fat Emet*, taught, "The commandments, the mitzvot, are like a candle—they can help remove the cover of ordinariness that darkens our world and help us recover the extraordinary that lies within every moment."

It is gratefulness that makes the heart great. (Abraham Joshua Heschel} For which we say, a hundred times, forever, amen and amen.

Spiritual Practice / Rituals

For noticing/doing something for the first time in your life, for the first time in its season (e.g. the first raspberries of the summer; the candles of the first night of Hanukkah) or for elevating and blessing a special moment in your life.

בָּרוּךְ אַתָּה יְיָ אֱלֹהֵינוּ מֶלֶךְ הָעוֹלָם שֶׁהֶחֱיָנוּ וְקִיְּמָנוּ וְהִגִּיעָנוּ לַזְּמַן הַזֶּה

Baruch ata Adonai eloheinu melech ha-olam,
she-hecheyanu v'kiyimanu v'higiyanu lazman ha-zeh

Blessed are You, Source of the Universe,
Who has kept us in life and sustained us and brought us to this moment.

A Morning Prayer of Thanks

מוֹדֶה אֲנִי לְפָנֶיךָ מלך חַי וְקַיָּם שֶׁהֶחֱזַרְתָּ בִּי נִשְׁמָתִי בְּחֶמְלָה, רַבָּה אֱמוּנָתֶךָ

Modeh/modah ani l'fanecha, melech chai v'kayam
She-he-chezarta bi nishmati b'chemla, rabah emunatecha.

I give thanks to You, Eternal and living God, who in love and faithfulness has reawakened my soul within me.
Great is Your trust.

For Wonders of Nature

ON SEEING LIGHTNING

בָּרוּךְ אַתָּה יְיָ אֱלֹהֵינוּ מֶלֶךְ הָעוֹלָם עוֹשֶׂה מַעֲשֵׂה בְרֵאשִׁית

Baruch ata Adonai eloheinu melech ha-olam oseh ma'asei vreishiyt

Blessed are You, Source of the Universe,
Author of ongoing creation.

ON HEARING THUNDER

בָּרוּךְ אַתָּה יְיָ אֱלֹהֵינוּ מֶלֶךְ הָעוֹלָם
שֶׁכֹּחוֹ וּגְבוּרָתוֹ מָלֵא עוֹלָם

Baruch ata Adonai eloheinu melech ha-olam

she-kocho u-g'vurato malei olam

Blessed are You, Source of the Universe,

Whose power and might fill the universe.

ON SEEING A RAINBOW

בָּרוּךְ אַתָּה יְיָ אֱלֹהֵינוּ מֶלֶךְ הָעוֹלָם זוֹכֵר הַבְּרִית וְנֶאֱמָן בִּבְרִיתוֹ וְקַיָּם בְּמַאֲמָרוֹ

Baruch ata Adonai eloheinu melech ha-olam zocher ha-brit

Blessed are You, Source of the Universe,

Who remembers the covenant.

ON SEEING FLOWERING TREES

בָּרוּךְ אַתָּה יְיָ אֱלֹהֵינוּ מֶלֶךְ הָעוֹלָם שֶׁלֹּא חִסַּר בְּעוֹלָמוֹ דָּבָר
וּבָרָא בוֹ בְּרִיּוֹת טוֹבוֹת
וְאִילָנוֹת טוֹבִים לְהַנּוֹת בָּהֶם בְּנֵי אָדָם

Baruch ata Adonai eloheinu melech ha-olam

she-lo chisar b'olamo davar

Blessed are You, Source of the Universe,

in Whose world nothing is lacking, and Who created beautiful creatures and flowering trees for human beings to enjoy.

For Learning

בָּרוּךְ אַתָּה יְיָ אֱלֹהֵינוּ מֶלֶךְ הָעוֹלָם
שֶׁנָּתַן מֵחָכְמָתוֹ לְבָשָׂר וָדָם

Baruch ata Adonai eloheinu melech ha-olam
she-natan mei-chochmato l'vasar va-dam
Blessed are You, Source of the Universe,
Who shared Divine Wisdom with mortal creatures.

For the Pleasures of Various Foods

בָּרוּךְ אַתָּה יְיָ אֱלֹהֵינוּ מֶלֶךְ הָעוֹלָם הַמּוֹצִיא לֶחֶם מִן הָאָרֶץ

Baruch ata Adonai eloheinu melech ha-olam
hamotzi lechem min ha-aretz
Blessed are You, Source of the Universe,
Who causes bread to come forth from the earth.

בָּרוּךְ אַתָּה יְיָ אֱלֹהֵינוּ מֶלֶךְ הָעוֹלָם בּוֹרֵא פְּרִי הָעֵץ

Baruch ata Adonai eloheinu melech ha-olam borei pri ha-eitz
Blessed are You, Source of the Universe,
Creator of the fruit of the tree.

בָּרוּךְ אַתָּה יְיָ אֱלֹהֵינוּ מֶלֶךְ הָעוֹלָם בּוֹרֵא מִינֵי מְזוֹנוֹת

Baruch ata Adonai eloheinu melech ha-olam

borei minei m'zonot

Blessed are You, Source of the Universe,

Who creates all kinds of foods.

בָּרוּךְ אַתָּה יְיָ אֱלֹהֵינוּ מֶלֶךְ הָעוֹלָם שֶׁהַכֹּל נִהְיֶה בִּדְבָרוֹ

Baruch ata Adonai eloheinu melech ha-olam

she-hakol nihiye b'dvaro

Blessed are You, Source of the Universe,

through Whom all comes into being.

בָּרוּךְ אַתָּה יְיָ אֱלֹהֵינוּ מֶלֶךְ הָעוֹלָם בּוֹרֵא פְּרִי הָאֲדָמָה

Baruch ata Adonai eloheinu melech ha-olam borei pri ha-adama

Blessed are You, Source of the Universe,

Creator of the fruit of the earth.

The Grace after Meals

בָּרוּךְ אַתָּה יְיָ הַזָּן אֶת הַכֹּל

Baruch ata Adonai ha-zan et ha-kol.

Sustenance there is for all; none need ever lack, no being ever want for food. We bless You, Source of sustenance.

For Fragrance

בָּרוּךְ אַתָּה יְיָ אֱלֹהֵינוּ מֶלֶךְ הָעוֹלָם בּוֹרֵא מִינֵי בְשָׂמִים

Baruch ata Adonai eloheinu melech ha-olam
borei minei v'samim

Blessed are You, Source of the Universe,
Creator of fragrant spices.

For Life Moments

ON EXPERIENCING A PERSONAL MIRACLE

בָּרוּךְ אַתָּה יְיָ אֱלֹהֵינוּ מֶלֶךְ הָעוֹלָם שֶׁעָשָׂה לִי נֵס בַּמָּקוֹם הַזֶּה

Baruch ata Adonai eloheinu melech ha-olam
she-asa li nes ba-makom ha-zeh

Blessed are You, Source of the Universe,
Who made a miracle for me in this place.

ON HEARING GOOD NEWS

בָּרוּךְ אַתָּה יְיָ אֱלֹהֵינוּ מֶלֶךְ הָעוֹלָם הַטּוֹב וְהַמֵּטִיב

Baruch ata Adonai eloheinu melech ha-olam
ha-tov v'ha-meitiv.

Blessed are You, Source of the Universe, Source of good.

ON HEARING NEWS OF A DEATH

בָּרוּךְ אַתָּה יְיָ אֱלֹהֵינוּ מֶלֶךְ הָעוֹלָם דַּיַן הָאֱמֶת

Baruch ata Adonai eloheinu melech ha-olam dayan ha-emet.

Blessed are You, Source of the Universe,
Faithful Source of meaning.

FOR FIRST TIME EXPERIENCES AND LIFE ITSELF

בָּרוּךְ אַתָּה יְיָ אֱלֹהֵינוּ מֶלֶךְ הָעוֹלָם שֶׁהֶחֱיָנוּ וְקִיְּמָנוּ וְהִגִּיעָנוּ לַזְּמַן הַזֶּה

Baruch ata Adonai eloheinu melech ha-olam,
she-hecheyanu v'kiyimanu v'higiyanu lazman ha-zeh

Blessed are You, Source of the Universe,
Who has kept us in life and sustained us and brought
us to this moment.

מקום

Makom / The Presence
A LIFE OF OPENNESS
We are never alone

בכל-המקום אשר אזכיר את-שמי אבוא אליך וברכתיך

In every place [*makom*] where I cause My Name to be
mentioned I will come to you and bless you.

Exodus 20:21

ועשו לי מקדש ושכנתי בתוכם

Build Me a sanctuary, that I may dwell among them.

Exodus 25:6

One of the beautiful names for God/Eternal is Makom. 'Makom' means 'place'—in this case, the One Who is Stranger to No Place. Or, in the words of the kabbalists, "There is no place devoid of the Presence."

אין מקום פנוי מינא

Ein makom panuy minei.

We, however, sometimes need places and physical touchstones in which to remember and notice. We can elevate the spaces where we live—our homes, our apartments, our dorms, our senior residences. Our home is more than just a place to live; our home is a place of soul, of gratitude, of blessing, of connection. Entering—or leaving—as we cross the threshold, we carry our values and our integrity with us as we move from the private space of our homes into the public sphere. As we cross the threshold, we remember our promises of faithfulness.

Spiritual Practice / Ritual

Putting up a Mezuzah

Blessings

בָּרוּךְ אַתָּה יְיָ אֱלֹהֵינוּ מֶלֶךְ הָעוֹלָם אֲשֶׁר קִדְּשָׁנוּ בְּמִצְוֹתָיו וְצִוָּנוּ לִקְבּוֹעַ מְזוּזָה

Baruch ata Adonai eloheinu melech ha-olam
asher kidshanu b'mitzvotav v'tzivanu likbo'a mezuza.

Blessed are You, Source of the Universe,
Who has called us to holiness through the act of affixing a mezuzah.

בָּרוּךְ אַתָּה יְיָ אֱלֹהֵינוּ מֶלֶךְ הָעוֹלָם שֶׁהֶחֱיָנוּ וְקִיְּמָנוּ וְהִגִּיעָנוּ לַזְּמַן הַזֶּה

Baruch ata Adonai eloheinu melech ha-olam
she-hecheyanu v'kiyimanu v'higiyanu lazman ha-zeh

Blessed are You, Source of the Universe,
Who has given us life and sustained us and brought us to his moment.

A Prayer for the Home We Want to Nurture

May the door of this home be wide enough to receive all who hunger for love, all who are lonely for fellowship.
May it welcome all who have cares to unburden, thanks to express, hopes to nurture.
May the door of this home be narrow enough to shut out pettiness and pride, envy and enmity.
May its threshold be no stumbling block to young or straying feet.
May it be too high to admit complacency, selfishness and harshness.
May this home be, for all who enter, the doorway to a richer and more meaningful life.
(Adapted from Rabbi Sidney Greenberg)

צדקה

Tzedaka / Jewish Vulnerability and Destiny
A LIFE OF RESPONSE
Reaching beyond the self

The essence of Jewish religious thinking does not lie in entertaining a concept of God but in the ability to articulate a memory of moments of illumination by [God's] presence. Israel is not a people of definers but a people of witnesses.

Abraham Joshua Heschel

"Ye are My witnesses." Isaiah 43:10

בָּרוּךְ אַתָּה יְיָ אֱלֹהֵינוּ מֶלֶךְ הָעוֹלָם שֶׁעָשַׂנִי יִשְׂרָאֵל

Baruch ata Adonai she-asani Yisrael.

Blessed are You, for the gift of being a Jew.

What does it mean to be a Jew in this world? Can you remember a time when someone said something denigrating or hurtful, and you felt the need to speak up? How did that feel? Did it feel that you opened yourself, that you added even an edge of vulnerability? Being Jewish is not only what we believe or what we do; deeper than that, being Jewish is who we are. To be a Jew is to live with courage and to remember how vulnerable we have been. To be a Jew is to remind ourselves that a society that is not safe for Jews will not be safe for anyone. As we fight for a world of religious freedom, for human and civil rights for ourselves, we also fight that battle for everyone. As we persist and celebrate our right to worship differently, eat differently, celebrate differently, we champion a society that recognizes and honors human diversity and uniqueness.

We have spoken truth to power. Whether it is Moses facing off against Pharaoh, or Natan Sharansky against the Soviet Empire, or common Jewish tailors and seamstresses who united against oppressive work conditions, fighting for economic justice, or challenging our leaders to do that which is just and right, to be a Jew is to speak truth to power.

We start by claiming our Jewishness.

Baruch ata Adonai.

Thank You for the gift of being a Jew.

When we come to die and stand before our Creator, our sages teach, we will be asked several questions. The last of them is: *Kivita la-yeshua* - did you hope for a better world? To be a Jew is to hope—to dream of a better world and rise to create it.

Spiritual Practice / Ritual

Belong to others. Find a community. Join a synagogue. Create a giving circle. Volunteer. Help to build a caring community. Reaching beyond the self requires a world to reach out to. You will find others, sharing in friendship and covenantal obligation, committed to the work of justice. We have known the heart of the stranger—and the vulnerability we know and remember propels us together to help create a more compassionate and just world.

Celebration

The comedian Henny Youngman once quipped, "I would be an atheist, but they have lousy holidays."

Belonging to a Jewish community also brings celebration—the chance to bring to life the stories of our people and to celebrate the values that animate a Jewish life, chief among them:

- Rosh Hashanah and Yom Kippur: Healing and return, reconciliation and second chances

- Hanukkah: The right to be different, celebrating religious diversity and uniqueness

- Purim: Translating Jewish vulnerability into acts of courage; masquerade and laughter
- Passover: The force of God moves through liberation; seek justice

A by-product of living life in this way is that we will build a framework for living, a way to walk the path of life.

A most favorite personal ad that we spotted in the classified section of a local Jewish newspaper read as follows:

"Retired gentleman seeks vital older woman to marry, to go to shul with, make Shabbos with, build a sukkah and celebrate Hanukkah with. Religion not important."

Thinking about life isn't as important when life itself already makes sense.

Belong to others. Find a community and strengthen it.

Spiritual Practice / Ritual

There is a blessing that is recited during weekday prayers, a prayer that reminds us of a universe in which compassionate justice will prevail. It can be recited while putting coins in a *tzedaka* charity box—or as you click and send donations to the causes you support.

בָּרוּךְ אַתָּה יְהֹוָה אֹהֵב צְדָקָה וּמִשְׁפָּט

Baruch ata Adonai, ohev tzedaka u'mishpat
Blessed are You, Source of the Universe,
Who loves *tzedakah* and justice.

שבת

Shabbat / Heaven on Earth
A LIFE OF JOY
Celebrating this moment

Shabbat is the celebration of Judaism's most essential values, an extraordinary and accessible pairing of spiritual wisdom with behavior and ritual. It is true: those who observe the Shabbat will be blessed with joy.

And it all comes together, the sevenfold path, the journey, the hard week, the anxieties, as the sun sets and Shabbat can enter our lives. There is a place where we can become one with the universe, where each step on the way blends into the next:

- **Tzelem Elohim / A Spark of the Divine**
  Each of us is worth celebrating.

- **Brit / Covenant**

  Learning to love; Shabbat is the celebration of covenantal love.

  We bless our family and friends.

- **Teshuvah / Healing and Return**

  Shabbat brings us back; it restores our soul.

  Some people seek forgiveness, clear the air and apologize before lighting Shabbat candles.

- **Kedusha / Nourishing a Heart of Gratitude**

  We slow down, we take time to bless.

  Light candles, drink wine, break bread.

- **Makom / Sacred Space**

  In the days when the Temple stood in Jerusalem, the Temple and its altars were the center of Jewish religious life. Since the destruction of the Second Temple two thousand years ago, the center of Jewish life has moved to the home. Our homes are sacred places and our table is the altar. As fancy as the Temple of old may have been, its altar was built out of rough unhewn stones. Any tool sharp enough to chisel and shape a stone could double as a tool of violence. No tool of violence could shape the altar.

  Since our homes are the temple and our table is the altar, we remind ourselves that our homes and our table need to be places of peace—a sacred place. After reciting *motzi*, the blessing over the bread, instead of using a knife, many people literally break bread—breaking off pieces of challah with their hands.

- **Tzedaka / Reaching Beyond the Self**
  Shabbat is meant to be a money-free zone, a time when we are less distracted by things and by commerce and consumption. Many people put money into a tzedaka box as they prepare to bring in Shabbat—or at Shabbat's end, with the ceremony of Havdalah.
  Invite someone to share a Shabbat meal with you.
  This is a meal not to be rushed. Take time to talk about things that matter.
  We have a culture rich in music and Shabbat table songs. Have you ever been envious of Irish folks gathering in pubs to share music and sing, or Americans on the country and bluegrass music trails, gathering on front porches with their instruments? We have that, too.

Spiritual Practice / Ritual

Candles: We light first and then bless (some pause before the blessing—a quiet and meditative moment—ushering in the serenity of this time).

בָּרוּךְ אַתָּה יְיָ אֱלֹהֵינוּ מֶלֶךְ הָעוֹלָם אֲשֶׁר קִדְּשָׁנוּ בְּמִצְוֹתָיו וְצִוָּנוּ לְהַדְלִיק נֵר שֶׁל שַׁבָּת

Baruch ata Adonai eloheinu melech ha-olam
asher kidshanu b'mitzvotav v'tzivanu l'hadlik ner shel Shabbat
Blessed are you, Source of the Universe,
Who calls us to holiness through the lighting of
the Shabbat candles.

Wine (or grape juice): We raise our glasses and sing together:

בָּרוּךְ אַתָּה יְיָ אֱלֹהֵינוּ מֶלֶךְ הָעוֹלָם בּוֹרֵא פְּרִי הַגָּפֶן

Baruch ata Adonai eloheinu melech ha-olam borei pri hagafen.

Blessed are You, Eternal our God, Source of the universe,
Creator of the fruit of the vine.

Bread/Challah: Say together—and then break bread.

בָּרוּךְ אַתָּה יְיָ אֱלֹהֵינוּ מֶלֶךְ הָעוֹלָם הַמּוֹצִיא לֶחֶם מִן הָאָרֶץ

*Baruch ata Adonai eloheinu melech ha-olam
hamotzi lechem min ha-aretz*

Blessed are You, Source of the Universe,
Who causes bread to come forth from the earth.

B'tayavon! Bon appetit!

Shabbat Blessing for Family and Friends

If there are children present, every child is held and blessed.

Yet, we all need to be held and told that we are loved—partners, friends, our family. Everyone at the table can be blessed. Place your arms around the person next to you as you say:

יְבָרֶכְךָ יְיָ וְיִשְׁמְרֶךָ

Yivarechicha Adonai v'yishmirecha

May God bless you and watch over you

יָאֵר יְיָ פָּנָיו אֵלֶיךָ וִיחֻנֶּךָּ

Ya-er Adonai panav eilecha viy'chuneka

May the light of God's grace shine on you

יִשָּׂא יְיָ פָּנָיו אֵלֶיךָ וְיָשֵׂם לְךָ שָׁלוֹם

Yisa Adonai panav eilecha v'yasem l'cha shalom

May God be with you and bless you with peace.

Havdalah—Saying Goodbye

Shabbat is so precious that we make a big deal about saying goodbye. With nightfall on Saturday night, we light a braided candle, pour a glass of wine and prepare fragrant spices (we use a spice box set aside for Havdalah.)

The simple and short ceremony includes blessings for taste, fragrance and sight. Adding beautiful song (sound) and the embrace of friends (touch), we have a short celebration of all five sensory senses.

Perhaps there is a sixth sense, an awareness that all of life is infused with the holy. The closing blessing of Havdalah is a reminder that imbedded within ordinary moments is a spark of the holy. Havdalah reminds us of our capacity to transform an ordinary moment into the extraordinary—from the mundane to the holy. All it takes is setting aside time, faithfully, and to notice the gift. We are each given the same moment. It is on us to notice it and rejoice in it.

Havdalah Blessings

בָּרוּךְ אַתָּה יְיָ אֱלֹהֵינוּ מֶלֶךְ הָעוֹלָם בּוֹרֵא פְּרִי הַגָּפֶן

Baruch ata Adonai Eloheinu melech ha-olam, borei pri hagafen.

Blessed are You, Eternal our God, Source of the universe,
Creator of the fruit of the vine.

בָּרוּךְ אַתָּה יְיָ אֱלֹהֵינוּ מֶלֶךְ הָעוֹלָם בּוֹרֵא מִינֵי בְשָׂמִים

Baruch ata Adonai Eloheinu melech ha-olam,
borei minei v'samim.

Blessed are You, Eternal our God, Source of the universe,
Creator of all manner of spices.

בָּרוּךְ אַתָּה יְיָ אֱלֹהֵינוּ מֶלֶךְ הָעוֹלָם בּוֹרֵא מְאוֹרֵי הָאֵשׁ

Baruch ata Adonai Eloheinu melech ha-olam, borei m'orei ha-eish.

Blessed are You, Eternal our God, Source of the universe,
Creator of the lights of the fire.

בָּרוּךְ אַתָּה יְיָ הַמַּבְדִיל בֵּין קֹדֶשׁ לְחֹל

Baruch ata Adonai hamavdil bein kodesh l'chol.

Blessed are You, Eternal our God, Source of the universe,
Who separates the sacred from the ordinary.

שָׁבוּעַ טוֹב

Shavu-a tov

A good week. A week of peace. May gladness
reign and joy increase.

We Are All Travelers, Walking the Path

The life-giving waters of Jewish wisdom flow beneath our feet, right where we live. We need a way to draw up these waters—a way to hold them—in order to irrigate and nourish our lives. Rituals are the vessels we use to draw up and channel these life-giving waters. The rituals—the practice—the doing—of Jewish living are the vessels that draw water from the well.

They help shape a life of purpose and belonging, of love and reconciliation, of courage and agency, faithfulness and joy.

"It is very close to you. It is in your mouth and in your heart and you can do it."

NOTES

Introduction

1. Siegel, B. *Love, Medicine and Miracles*, pp. 130–31.
2. Meyerhoff, B. *Number Our Days*, pp. 38–39.
3. Kushner, L. *Honey from the Rock*, p. 16.
4. Plaut, W. G. *The Torah—A Modern Commentary*, pp. xxxvii–xxxviii.
5. Quoted in Jancee Dunn, "We Asked for Your Offbeat Holiday Traditions," *New York Times*, November 29, 2024.

Chapter 1

1. Twerski, A. *Life's Too Short*, pp. 2–3.

Chapter 2

1. Wiman, C. *My Bright Abyss*, p. 70.
2. Remen, R. *My Grandfather's Blessings: Stories of Strength, Refuge, and Belonging*, pp. 1–2.
3. "The U.S. Economy Is Racing Ahead. Almost Everything Else Is Falling Behind," *New York Times*, February 3, 2025.
4. Peck, S. *The Road Less Traveled: A New Psychology of Love, Traditional Values, and Spiritual Growth*, p. 84.
5. Elcott, D. *A Sacred Journey: The Jewish Quest for a Perfect World*, p. 107.
6. Miller, M., *Oprah*, February 2006, https://www.oprah.com/omagazine/getting-over-disappointment-in-a-relationship/5.

Chapter 3

1. Twerski, A. *Life's Too Short*, pp. 162–63.
2. https://www.theforgivenessproject.com/stories.
3. Nachman of Bratislav. *Likutei Moharan* 282.
4. Telushkin, J. *The Book of Jewish Values*, Day 193, p. 277.
5. Ibid., p. 278.
6. "The 'F' Word: Images of Forgiveness—Catalogue for the Exhibit." Interviews by Marina Cantacuzino and photography by Brian Moody, theforgivenessproject.com.
7. Berry, J. The Forgiveness Project, https://www.theforgivenessproject.com/stories.
8. Maimonides. *Mishneh Torah*, Hilchot Teshuva 5:2.
9. Stern, S. "Visions of an Alternative Rabbinic Journey," *CCAR Journal*, Winter 2011.
10. Feinstein, E. "Cultivating Hope," *Sefaria*, https://www.sefaria.org/sheets/267753?lang=bi.

Chapter 4

1. Schulweis, H. *In God's Mirror*, p. 136.

Chapter 5

1. Casals, P. *Joys and Sorrows*, p. 17.

Chapter 6

1. Rittner, C., and Myers, S. *Courage to Care*, pp. 24–25.

INDEX

Barrett Browning, Elizabeth 14

Cordovero, Moses 99

Delancey Street 29–30

Halakha 15
Heschel AJ 128
Holocaust 25, 64, 71, 118

Kabbalah 99
Kabbalists 43, 98, 109
Kotzker Rebbe 50, 53
Kristallnacht 51–52

Melchior, Michael 25
Meyerhoff, Barbara 3
Mezuzah 110
Miller, Michael Vincent 34, 40
Mishnah 23, 25–26

Mitzvah 35, 45–46, 84

Nachman of Bratislav xiii, 56, 65, 75, 93
Norton, Michael 15

Rathenau, Walter 68–70

Schindler's List 25
Shabbat xi, xiii, 17, 24, 45–46, 54, 81–82, 93, 103, 121, 125–133, 135, 137, 139
Siegel, Bernie 1

Talmud 36, 50
Thich Nhat Hanh 43, 91
Twerski, Abraham 26–27, 55
Tzimtzum 99

Zohar 12

ABOUT THE AUTHORS

Shira Milgrom served as rabbi of the Congregation Kol Ami in White Plains, New York, for thirty-seven years, building a community of activism, joy, and spiritual courage. As a rabbi and community leader, she pioneered notable events that brought the Black and Jewish and multiple faith communities together in common purpose. She has also played an active role in helping to resettle Syrian immigrants, promoting Israeli-Palestinian dialogue and American Jewish-Muslim dialogue, and making Kol Ami an LGBTQ-friendly spiritual community. Known as a powerful speaker and thought leader, she reflects a generation of rabbis who passionately create extraordinary encounters with Jewish texts, rituals, and traditions that merge the intimate and personal with a grand vision of the Jewish people.

David Elcott, author and professor, has spent decades at the intersection of community building, the search for a theology of cross-boundary engagement, and interfaith social justice organizing and activism. Trained in political psychology at Columbia University and Judaic studies at the American Jewish University, Dr. Elcott retired as the Taub Professor of Practice at NYU Wagner to be a Senior Fellow at Columbia University's Center for Justice, teaching incarcerated men studying in prison for their college degree. He is author of *On the Significance of Religion in Immigration Policy* (with

Barnabas Aspray, 2025), *Faith, Nationalism and the Future of Liberal Democracy* (with C. Colt Anderson, Tobias Cremer, and Volker Haarmann, 2021), and *A Sacred Journey: The Jewish Quest for a Perfect World* (1995). Dr. Elcott has traveled the world as an interfaith mediator and disciple of social justice activism. He has been in the media and published extensively as a scholar who analyzes the nexus of politics, society, and religious fervor.